# Advertising Impression Measurement

### Inside the Cross-Platform Revolution Changing the Industry

by

Edward E. Smallwood, Ph.D.

## Dedication

I dedicate this book to my lovely wife, Sondra. You have been my constant support and cheerleader. Your love has sustained me. Your praise has motivated me. Thank you, my angel.

## Acknowledgments

John Donne observed in 1624 that "no man is an island." That observation applies to many areas of life -- and certainly to book-length works. I am grateful for all of those who have challenged me, taught me, and enlightened me along the road to this book.

I wish to thank Larry W. Long, Ph.D., who served as my advisor at N.C. State University and who led me to a master's program at Illinois State University. Larry, you've been an inspiration and a trusted advisor; I can always count on you.

From Regent University, I want to acknowledge the guidance of Drs. John Keeler, William Brown, and Stephen Perry. Your wisdom and assistance were immensely helpful in crafting this idea into a fully-developed treatise.

Finally, I wish to express my sincere appreciation to the participants of this study who volunteered valuable time to share their opinions, their expertise, and their visions of advertising. Without them, this book could never have been.

# Contents

# Chapter 1

**Advertising Lacks a Cross-Platform Delivery Measure**

This first chapter discusses the importance of advertising and the need for a cross-platform delivery measure, with a brief introduction, followed by the declared purpose of the study. Next, this chapter presents the background of the problem and lays out four specific needs for this study.

**Introduction**

Advertising is pervasive in the western world. In fact, most Americans take advertising for granted as a common part of life. We simply expect that our television and radio entertainment will have advertising. We further expect that our magazines and newspapers will have advertising. Billboards and other forms of outdoor advertising have long been part of our cultural landscape. Even our sports teams and live events depend on advertising as an integral part of their funding, distribution, and branding models. Advertising populates the Internet and related digital technology forms. Our mobile devices, apps, and social media have become platforms for advertising and other types of promotion.

The scale of advertising in the western world is staggering. Americans, in particular, are literally awash in advertising. We live in advertised homes, eat advertised cereal for breakfast, drive in advertised cars, enjoy advertised restaurants, play in advertised tennis shoes with advertised toys, view advertised movies, and brush our teeth with advertised toothpaste – and toothbrushes – before going to sleep in our advertised beds on advertised mattresses. Indeed, contemporary America reflects, and is shaped by, advertising – and life would seem odd without it.

Increasingly, advertising has become integrated into many aspects of modern life.  In fact, "encountering advertising is a daily occurrence for most people" (Duff & Faber, 2011, p.51).  In today's world, it is even more common than a daily occurrence for many.  Estimates vary widely, but Lamoureux (2016) reports that people are exposed to a range of between 247 and up to 20,000 advertising messages daily!  Elsen, Pieters, and Wedel (2016) assert the number is several thousand daily ads.  While the current scope may be accelerated due to media proliferation, the importance of advertising is not a new trend; advertising is also significant from a historical perspective.  "The social history preserved in advertisements is like an archaeological record" (O'Barr, 2005, para. 5).  Advertising messages and imagery help establish and reflect social standards for influence, values, normality, and what is cool (Taylor, 2009; Jenkins, 2013).  Because of the relevance of the topic, many scholars have studied advertising. In fact, the Academic Search Complete database reports more than 200,000 academic journal articles dealing with the topic (EBSCOHost, 2016).  Soley and Reid (1983) found that nearly 2,000 articles focusing on advertising were published in just 16 journals in the U.S. alone in a recent decade.  Kim, Hayes, Avant, and Reid (2014) observed that journals from many fields and disciplines publish advertising research; however, they found that no less than 17 academic journals publish the predominance of advertising research.  A Google Scholar search (2016) revealed more than one million books and articles on the topic since just 2010.

One inescapable result of advertising's omnipresence, both historically and today, is that it is an enormous business with a huge financial footprint.  Aaker & Norris (1982) claim that advertising should be studied because "advertising contributes to the health and vitality of the economic system" (p.61).  According to Thorson and Rodgers (2012), "Advertising is acknowledged as the engine that drives consumer purchasing and, therefore, advertising 'keeps the wheels of the economy turning'" (p. 10).  A Pivotal Research Group forecast reported that U.S. advertising expenditures across media reached more than $203 billion in 2016 (Inside Radio, 2017).  Worldwide, advertising agency Zenith Media estimated global advertising expenditures exceeded $539 billion in 2016 (Performics, 2016).

Further, the number of advertising vehicles available has virtually exploded in the twenty-first century.  No longer do advertisers or their agencies have to consider only the traditional "mass" media of newspapers, magazines, radio, and television.  Now they must also consider cable television, websites, Netflix, mobile, Google, YouTube, Facebook, Twitter, Instagram, SnapChat, video games, "apps" of all kinds, and an almost-endless universe of new media options that continues to expand.  These trends have stimulated even greater interest on the part of advertising organizations to find reliable methods of determining the best means of delivering advertising messages, as well as, the effectiveness of their advertising efforts.  While scholars have long been interested in advertising, advertising media, and advertising effects on individuals, audiences, and cultures, their research has tended to focus on the psychological aspects of concepts such as persuasion and/or engagement, the advertising creative process, or campaign strategies.  Formal, quantifiable, advertising measurement has received relatively little attention.  However, there are a number of different kinds of advertising measurements that have been used over the past century or so: from noting and the recall of Starch (1928) and advertising effects research of Lasswell, Lazarsfeld, et al. to galvanic skin reactions (Golin & Lyerly, 1950; Ohme, Reykowska,Wiener, & Choromanska, 2009), to engagement research (Gambetti & Graffigna, 2015; Kim, Lee, Jo, Jung, & Kang, 2015), to persuasion-based attitude change (McGuire, 1984; Cacciopo & Petty, 1984) to sales/revenue metrics, cost per point (CPP), and a host of others.  The present challenge in the industry is to develop and examine a single measure of delivery for advertising messages that can be applied across all media.

Meanwhile, there remains a significant dearth of scholarship conducted in the realm of delivery measurement.  The concept of measurement of delivery focuses quite simply on whether the message was actually delivered to a target audience member and then counts the resultant impressions.  An impression can be thought of as a single exposure to a given message.  Ross, Ostroff, and Jernigan (2016) define an advertising impression as "a measure of advertising exposure, representing a single ad seen by a single viewer" (Methods, para. 2).  Research dealing with measuring advertising delivery is needed in an era with so many varied forms of media and media platforms.  The impression is a critical component of advertising delivery.  This study will help fill a void by exploring advertising industry leaders' perceptions of cross-platform advertising methods of measuring delivery and other new approaches that may be better suited to today's advertising and media environment.

**Purpose of the Study**

The specific purpose of this study was to discover perspectives from a variety of advertising experts regarding the need for, nature of, and potential effectiveness of a cross-platform measure of advertising delivery: the impression.  Using a qualitative research approach that will be described in Chapter 3, the study will solicit the opinions of these diverse experts about their past and current experiences with existing advertising measurement systems and tools.  Their ideas about what should be considered when developing a more effective impression-based, holistic, industry-metric suitable for the current and future advertising and digital media environment and their insights about other trends that may influence the ways and measures of advertising effectiveness, are created and used.  The goal is to integrate the opinions of these experts to evaluate a system of advertising measurement that addresses the need for consideration of how well advertising has been delivered -- in the context of advertising efforts that are increasingly multi-media platform in character when attempting to reach target markets or audiences who increasingly make use of many different forms of media or their applications. Note that this is not a technical feasibility study; rather, it is an evaluation of cross-platform metrics by representatives from the advertising industry.  In addition to ideas suggested by the participants, the advertising impression (exposure to an advertising message) will be evaluated with regard to the advantages and disadvantages of the cost per thousand (CPM) impression measurement approach from multiple viewpoints within the professional advertising space.  This concept will be referred to as advertising impression measurement (AIM).

**Background of Problem**

Because huge sums of financial resources are spent on advertising, businesses, and non-profit organizations of all types that use advertising, as well as the advertising agencies that support them, there is a demand that the measurement of advertising keep up with trends in the media landscape.  Television has long been considered the most dominant advertising medium in the United States as it impacts the lives of virtually all Americans. Yet, even the behemoth that is television advertising is not immune to change.  CEO of cable TV and media giant Comcast, Brian Roberts, predicted in 2012 that "television will change more in the next five years than it has in the past 50" (Pearlstine, 2012, para. 2).  The broad adoption of streaming video services, such as Netflix and Amazon Prime, in addition to the cable company "OnDemand" offerings has had significant impacts on television viewing and financial modeling.  Indeed, change is continuing in video consumption, even blurring the lines of what "television" actually is.  For example, YouTube has established content agreements with major talents such as Amy Poehler,

Tom Hanks, Madonna, Jay-Z, and Ashton Kutcher (Rosen, 2013).  Of course, mobile and tablets

have also impacted the way "television" is viewed – on non-television devices.  Further, even

linear programmers now sometimes offer all episodes of a season at once – allowing viewers to

binge or to watch on their own schedules.  (No more agonizing over the cliffhanger until next

week's exciting episode.)  Additionally, television is not just a competitor to new media but is

also considered part of the digital landscape as both continue to evolve (Mandese, 2016) or

converge.  As Roberts predicted, television today is starting to look a lot less like the television

of the past – with many cable companies and programmers offering their content on different

devices and in different ways.

Not only television, but virtually all media depend heavily on advertising as a primary

component of their revenue models.  As with other corporate or organizational activities,

advertising budgets and related resources have financial constraints and a concurrent demand for

accountability.  Therefore, advertisers look for comparative and performance metrics to justify

their spending as well as to evaluate and improve their advertising results.  For example, some

advertisers might be interested in a comparative metric to answer questions such as 'Which

media deliver better?' or 'Which media are more efficient?'  Another metric that advertisers

constantly strive to understand is advertising effectiveness.  However, advertising now exists

across many media types.  Consistent or clear measures of delivery and effectiveness are hard to

come by; further, interpretation of effectiveness is dependent upon advertising goals.

Complicating this issue is that a universally-accepted definition of advertising

effectiveness has not been established in the past.  For example, Starch (1928) proposed that

advertising effectiveness could be measured by noting or ad recall from people exposed to the

ads.  Campbell (1965) suggested market share as a measure of advertising effectiveness.

Krugman (1966) articulated the concept of involvement (aka engagement) as another measure of advertising – and that theme continues to be studied by others – although there remains a lack of agreement regarding the concept (Heath, 2009; Paine, 2009; Mersey, Malthouse, & Calder, 2010; and Tsiotsou, 2013). Matricon (1967) recommended an index of advertising effectiveness arguing that "advertising which improves brand attitudes of an individual with low probability of seeing the ad is more effective than advertising which produces the same effect on an individual with high exposure probability" (p. 33).

Some have suggested that advertising effectiveness should be measured by sales or profits (Hise & Strawser, 1976). However, Politz argued that "sales success or failure does not prove success or failure of advertising" (1975, p, 10). Advertising measures also include a host of sometimes arcane concepts that are even more difficult to define, such as brand value (Stone & Duffy, 1993). Brand value is somewhat similar to "trademark equity" (p. 11) and indicates the overall value of the brand. Of course, reach and frequency have long been standard measures in advertising (Headen, Klompmaker, & Teel, 1976; Danaher, 2007), although they do not deal with effectiveness per se. Instead, they primarily deal with *estimated* delivery. More recently, Danaher and Dagger (2013) measured purchase incidence as an indicator of advertising effectiveness. They define purchase incidence as at least one visit to a retailer's store (either online or brick-and-mortar). Also, the concept of "effective frequency" has been considered as an important measure of advertising success (Kreshel, Lancaster, & Toomey, 1985; Cannon, 2012; Schmidt & Eisend, 2015). Effective frequency is considered the "number of advertising exposures that leads to optimal consumer response regarding attitudes and recall" (Schmidt & Eisend, 2015, p. 425). However, optimal consumer response is open to widely variable interpretations.

Sheth (1974) observed that "theorizing about advertising effectiveness is analogous to the eternal search for inner peace, everybody hopes for it, some attempt to search for it, but no one has yet discovered it" (p. 6). Yet the quest continues. Media and advertising practitioners have also developed proprietary models to measure engagement or "the degree to which the creative content and media context of any marketing communications results in meaningful communications regarding the brand" (Marich, 2008, p. 12). Unfortunately, for the advertising industry, the concept of effectiveness remains somewhat akin to the old adage "beauty is in the eye of the beholder."

So where do we go from here? If it can be measured, effectiveness can only be gauged in retrospect. And sometimes the time-lag required for reporting figures such as sales or long-term advertising effects can significantly delay feedback loops. However, when advertisers and agencies plan and prepare advertising campaigns, they need to have information regarding comparative delivery metrics to optimize spending allocations and message distribution in a timely manner. Further, the focus on effectiveness merely assumes that the messages have been delivered; yet, without measurement of said delivery, the delivery cannot be confirmed, quantified, or evaluated.

Advertising and other forms of marketing, communication, and public relations have been historically both "planned and measured on a medium-by-medium basis, yet it is indisputable that modern consumers consume many, if not all, of these communication media concurrently" (Reinold & Tropp, 2012, p. 119). Viljakainen (2013) refers to this differentiated, media-specific method as the *silo* approach – and reports that it is the approach used almost exclusively by both practitioners and scholars. (The terms 'silo,' 'siloed,' or 'siloization' are used hereafter to refer to media and measurement that are separated and disconnected – that function as standalone entities despite the widespread use of cross-platform/multimedia advertising.)  She argues that the entrenched systems of media and measurement are resisting the shift to more holistic measurement alternatives.  This resistance presents an obstacle for advertisers and marketers who desire to maximize their usage of media to get the proper messages to their appropriate targets effectively and efficiently.  More than 50 years ago, Christian and Ochs (1966) observed "the need for comparable audience data has never before been fulfilled" (p. 59) though they argued that the concept should receive attention.

Measurement and reporting tools do exist for lots of media, but they continue to be separate and *unconnected* in the marketplace; Franz (2000) bemoaned "we live in a multi-source media research world" (p. 461).  Multiple practitioners in the industry have acknowledged and complained about the lack of cross-platform metrics.  For example, Winslow (2013) reported in an issue of *Broadcasting & Cable*:

> TV uses very different measures of usage than those found in the digital world, making it difficult if not impossible to add up total viewing for a show across TV, online, mobile, social media and other digital platforms.  The result, some researchers complain, is a morass of incompatible data that is forcing them to create what several call, "Frankenmetrics."
>
> "It's been called Frankenmetrics because we are getting arms and legs and heads from different places that have to be sewn together," says Jack Wakshlag, chief research officer at Turner Entertainment.  "Unfortunately, the result really isn't a whole functioning entity."  "Fixing this is the most important issue facing the industry right now," adds Alan Wurtzel, president of research and media development for NBCUniversal.

This is particularly important as viewing continues to fragment over multiple devices, explains CBS chief research officer David Poltrack. The confusion surrounding multiplatform measurement also impacts a variety of other players, including ad agencies and media buyers. 'We are chomping at the bit over here,' says Jordan Bitterman, chief strategy officer of [Ad Agency] Mindshare North America. 'The media and marketing industry is definitely thirsting for crossplatform campaigns and measurement.' 'You have a Tower of Babel with incompatible systems,' says Brian Wieser, senior research analyst at Pivotal Research Group.

Better cross-platform research will also require advertisers, agencies and major industry execs from the television, online and mobile world to agree on common terms for defining that usage, which is challenging given the different nature of usage across these media. Most TV players would like to see a currency based on gross ratings points (GRP); others believe it will be impressions, preferring to see TV ratings mirror the currency of online measurement. Not surprisingly, the model battle reflects the needs of each side. (p. 12-13)

As indicated earlier, the lack of agreement about advertising effectiveness is likely related to the highly subjective nature of the concept. Whether advertising is successful in its goals – or not – depends on what the goals are and how they are defined – or often, if goals even exist. According to Faber, Duff, and Nan (2012), "the first goal of advertising is to gain attention" (p. 26). An additional advertising goal might be to get noticed; another goal might be to earn name recognition; still another goal might be to build a brand; and, a further goal might be to increase sales. Marketers have long held that the end goal of advertising is to stimulate sales (Lavidge & Steiner, 2000).  Alas, all these goals would require different measures for effectiveness – or a system of measures that satisfies all of them.

Another critical element in advertising is the target audience.  It is common practice in the advertising profession to define target audiences carefully then create and deliver advertising messages in ways that are tailored to these audiences to meet advertising goals.  The target audience is those people who are prospects for whatever it is the advertiser is selling, e.g., the product, service, or idea (Levinson, 1994).  In other words, advertising messages are not just broadcast into the stratosphere (or cyberspace); rather, they are designed to tell a specific story, or communicate a particular attribute, to a person or group of people who fall into a category which the advertiser has identified as containing potential consumers.  Cannon (2012) is much more specific; he describes the people that are *reached* by advertising messages as the *audience.* Meanwhile, the *target audience* is those people who represent the practical, boots-on-the-ground translation of the target market (usually for media selection/evaluation purposes).  For example, if an advertiser is selling tennis balls, people who play tennis would be part of the larger, conceptual target market – but in order to use specific media to reach those people, advertisers might send messages to sports enthusiasts (on ESPN or in *Sports Illustrated*), or perhaps even men 18-34.

Unfortunately, for advertisers, media continue to be measured separately and individually – on scales developed primarily *for* those particular media *and* to the exclusion of other media. Multiple measurement organizations have essentially laid vertical claim to various media and often provide virtually monopolistic or at least 'semi-exclusive' delivery metrics for a given media.  For example, Nielsen Media Research is the dominant player in the television ratings industry; it provides ratings as a percentage of a designated market area or DMA.  Arbitron (though now part of Nielsen) is the dominant player in the radio industry; it provides ratings as a percentage of a different geographic construct -- the area of dominant influence or ADI.  A handful of research companies specialize in newspaper research; Scarborough and Simmons (and to a lesser extent, International Demographics) are examples from this market.  Various syndicated research companies, such as Mediamark Research Incorporated, Claritas, and others offer lifestyle and segmentation (or cluster) studies that include elements of behavior, demographics, product usage, and media exposure.  There are few research companies that offer syndicated reporting to reflect the landscape of in-game advertising or sports sponsorships.  Meanwhile, RenTrak historically measured motion pictures – even though films are not normally considered "ad-supported" – but now the company has evolved into online measurement.  Google Analytics, owing partly to the company's 2007 purchase of DoubleClick, is now one of the major players in web measurement, along with Comscore (Rentrak).  However, the online market is highly fragmented, and there are a significant number of players.  Many digital publishers provide their own research measurement for advertisers; Facebook is one of the notable companies in this latter group.  In addition, streaming services such as Netflix and Amazon's Prime Video also provide their own delivery metrics.  Advertisers typically lack verifiable data and must simply trust (hope and pray) that the numbers are valid.  However, throughout advertising history, those who purchase advertising have shown a clear preference for a 'third party arbiter' of media delivery metrics (e.g., Nielsen or Arbitron) that can offer an element of impartiality.  McDonald (2008) put it this way:

> The advertising-supported media have functioned as three-way markets among
> media, consumers, and advertisers: the media have attracted audiences that they in
> turn have re-sold to advertisers. Media audience measurement companies have

been the neutral arbiters of the process, providing the 'currency' of exchange between media buyers and sellers. As such they have been responsible for verifying the size and composition of those media audiences, thereby rationalizing media planning and reducing friction in the marketplace. Because of the high cost of collecting data and the reluctance of market participants to accept multiple 'currencies' with differing values, there has tended to be only one single, dominant supplier of media audience data within each media sector (e,g., in the United States, Nielsen for TV, Arbitron for radio, MRI for magazines, etc.). (p. 315)

Again, the challenge for contemporary advertisers is that there is no consistent metric or measurement available to help them to assess relative effectiveness – or even delivery – among the plethora of media options.  As media outlets are highly competitive, they generally want to stay in their siloes and show little to no interest in supporting cross-platform measurement. (However, such positions may be changing as media entities cross over and provide content via multiple platforms.)  Further, the entrenched measurement monopolies (e.g., Nielsen, Arbitron, etc.) have proven reluctant to threaten or cannibalize their primary revenue streams in the industries they dominate by changing to accommodate other media effectively.

Of course, the confluence of media to which audiences are exposed results in overlapping user experiences that are often difficult to differentiate, much less measure discretely.  For example, if a viewer watches CNN on cable television, on an iPad, on a cell phone, or through a web browser from the CNN website, should those views count as television, computer, and mobile impressions individually – or collectively as some sort of 'converged media'?  Further, when someone reads an article on the *Sports Illustrated* website, should that be counted as a magazine impression or as an online exposure?  What if this person began reading the article in the paper magazine but then followed a link to the website to get more information…How should that be counted?  Imagine further if this 'reader' then watched a video on the sports topic in question from the *Sports Illustrated* website.  How should the video exposure be measured and/or compared?  Should these exposures be considered separately or in the context of the magazine?  Who decides what should be included or excluded?

Schultz, Block, and Raman (2009) further commented on the challenge of individual media stubbornly persisting with their separate measurement tools in seeming defiance of usage by consumers and as well as advertisers:

Multimedia understanding would seem to be critically important today, given that most distribution-based media measures are based on single media form identification, that is, television viewing is measured separately from radio listening, which is measured separately from magazine readership, which is measured separately from outdoor exposure and so on.  Today, even the newer forms of media, such as mobile, word-of mouth and even social media are also measured separately and individually with no regard for the simultaneous media consumption by the participating audiences. (p. 5)

The advertising industry is struggling for answers to these issues.  However, most media struggles with these hurdles individually, sometimes as individual companies.  Thus, the advertisers – the ones spending the money – are still left without a comparison metric for even the simplest measure: message delivery.  Not only is delivery one of the simplest concepts, it is also arguably a precursor to all other measures of advertising effectiveness.  The academic community has an opportunity to contribute to this discussion for both practitioners and scholars by proposing and studying potential solutions to the measurement morass.

**Need for Scholarly Research**

The trends and issues described in the previous sections suggest a need for scholarly research. This study responds to that need by addressing four basic challenges associated with this opportunity. First, there is a need for scholarly studies that deal with cross-platform advertising measurement within the industry and possible ways to conduct it effectively. Second, there is a recognized disconnect between scholars and practitioners of advertising. There is a need for studies that can span this divide. Third, there have been calls for scholarship dealing with improved measurement. Finally, there is also a paucity of advertising studies that focus on advertising message delivery in particular. Each of these challenges is discussed in the following sections.

**Cross-platform ad measurement.** As has been described in previous sections, in addition to delivery, advertising has also been measured in regard to engagement, sales, impressions, ratings, recall, effectiveness, and other attributes. There are evolving and increasing numbers of advertising channels and multiple measures of advertising delivery and effectiveness. Businesses and organizations are aware of these changes in the media landscape, even as commercial measurement has failed to keep pace. Academic research concerned with these changes has not kept pace either. As McDonald (2008) noted, advertisers are "breaking out of silos, planning cross platform campaigns that frequently mix traditional media with PR activities, sponsorships, events, product placements, and other forms of promotion" (p. 316). But how do advertisers measure their cross-platform advertising delivery? Most major media (and advertising presented in them) are measured independently and often use metrics that do not translate across competing – or even complementary – media.  There appears to be a growing industry-wide appetite for a metric that can be applied to multiple media.  For example, an advertising industry organization, Coalition for Innovative Media Measurement (CIMM), has identified eight criteria necessary for cross-platform media measurement.  One of the organization's key criteria is that "common metrics are needed to make comparisons of exposure across platforms" (2015).

Scholars have also observed the need for metrics that apply across multiple media.  "The practice of media has been changing for some time, most recently including the growth of social media, technologies that put the viewer in more control, the introduction of screens of different types and, with them, more interactivity" (Taylor et al., 2013, p. 200).  More than ever, marketers need data on media consumption that include all platforms (Smit & Neijens, 2011; Viljakainen, 2013).  Simply put: changes in media usage require changes in advertising measurement.  As media multiply, splinter, integrate, overlap, converge, and otherwise evolve, measurement to support advertising purchase decisions and evaluations must also evolve.  Baehr (2005) recommended "undertaking appropriate converged media research efforts" that "examine the media landscape collectively as it exists, determining the role of each media channel in this new media mix" (p. 135).  Baehr and others recognized that media are still different, and they retain their unique characteristics; however, advertisers need a reliable metric that at least answers the most basic question across media: was the ad seen (heard, noticed, etc.)?  In other words, advertising needs to coalesce around a simple measurement concept: message delivery.

Lancaster, Kreshel, and Harris (1986) observed that "one of the most fundamental concerns of advertising media planning theory and practice is developing and evaluating media schedules in terms of advertising exposures" (p.26).  However, they argue that the practice is exceedingly difficult because media measurement is based on individual media options as no holistic measurement offerings exist.  Unfortunately, competing metrics that are used for particular media vehicles simply do not offer multi-media comparability.  In fact, the different measurement metrics currently in place almost seem designed to thwart multi-media comparison.  Advertisers have been encouraged to use a variety of communication forms for their campaigns and have had apparent success in doing so.  "Advertisers increasingly and successfully have used multiplatform communications to achieve synergistic results in getting messages across to consumers within a single marketing campaign" (Laroche, Kiani, Economakis, & Richard, 2013, p. 433).  However, to more accurately determine the effectiveness of these multi-media efforts, they need measurement across all of those media on a comparative basis (Smit & Neijens, 2011).

In 2008, the World Federation of Advertisers (WFA) introduced what it called a "blueprint for consumer-centric holistic measurement" in which it listed goals for future audience measurement.  The blueprint called for consistent information and measurement to get superior insights on multi-media behavior.  However, the WFA warned that disparate data sets will hinder multimedia measurement.  Unfortunately, disparate data sets are the norm as advertisers and media researchers still "tend to observe, investigate and measure advertising in splendid isolation" (Kerr & Schultz, 2010, p. 563).

Omni-channel advertising needs a common measurement system; unfortunately, the measurement industry still does not support that need.  Meanwhile, the need continues to increase based on advertiser usage, consumer demand, and media proliferation.  "Cross-channel advertising has grown steadily and significantly as a means to reach consumers.  Television, the Internet, and other channels are used together to market products" (Laroche, Kiani, Economakis,

& Richard, 2013, p. 431).  Consulting firms also realize the need continues to increase but with no well-developed solution in sight.  "Although omnichannel marketing is a primary goal for the majority of marketers, executing on that strategy is proving to be a challenge," (Forrester, 2015, p. 3).  From an academic perspective, Viljakainen (2013) echoes this contention, "there is a need for a common language in media buying and media selling" (p. 58).  The practitioner perspective is even more direct "'The No. 1 conundrum hitting clients on both sides of the equation, agencies and media companies, is how to handle video in an omni [or multiplatform] environment,' says Sarah Foss, president of the advertising division for digital distributor Yangaroo" (Winslow, 2014, p. 32).

Practitioners are dealing with the cross-platform challenge on a daily basis.  More and more, advertisers are looking for "fluid campaigns" or "flex campaigns" that offer the capability to move advertising impressions across media or platforms (Jerry Rocha, April 13, 2016, personal communication).  According to Chris Faw, Senior Vice President of Operations, Spectrum Reach, the national advertising sales firm NCC Media wants to be "prepared to deal with ALL impressions" regardless of media source (personal communication, April 25, 2015). In addition, major advertising agencies are also switching to impressions; "Universal-McCann, a global, full-service advertising agency (part of the Interpublic Group) and MediaOcean, a privately held advertising services and software company, announced in 2015 that they were switching from ratings to impressions as the primary measure of advertising delivery" (L. Rodriguez, personal communication, April 22, 2015).

Multiple media channels align with suggestions by researchers that multiple-source messages would be more easily processed by (and will motivate more) consumers than repetitive messages on the same old individual media.  Chang and Thorson (2004) advocate that marketers should apply a multiple-source strategy since presenting information in varied contexts leads to ad messages being encoded in slightly different ways, which enhances mental retrieval ability and therefore increases awareness.

According to Aitchison (2011),

> The use of multiple media to reach a target audience is common advertising practice. No longer content to rely solely on conventional high-reach media such as television, advertisers are using a mix of touchpoints, embracing everything from online, to tablets, to social media, to real-time in-store mobile communications. (as cited in Romaniuk, Beal, & Uncles, 2013, p. 221)

Nichols (2013) observed that "marketers commonly measure the performance of each of their marketing activities as if they work independently of one another—so called swim-lane measurement" (p. 2). He argues that such measurement fails to take into account the influence that ads can have on each other – across media. Rust and Oliver (1994), in a warning to the advertising industry, predicted that new media and technological changes would result in the fragmentation of both media and markets while simultaneously offering greater power and choice to consumers.

Kevin Roberts, CEO of advertising agency Saatchi & Saatchi, hit home with his observation more than a decade ago:

> Consumers know exactly what they want. They want it all. They want to read their news in the newspaper. They want a weekly magazine to give them a bit of perspective. They want updates on their mobile phones. They want to check out stuff on the Internet. They want to listen to the radio in their cars. They want big

pictures on their TVs in the evening. They're not remotely confused. (Tungate,

2007, p. 259)

Scholars continue to recognize and point out the changes to media and their impact on

advertising. "Profound changes in the media ecosystem mean renewed emphasis on multi-media

campaign efficiency and effectiveness" (Romaniuk, Beal, & Uncles, 2013, p. 221; Assael, 2011).

They recognize that media, and by extension, advertising, continue to expand in both

volume and complexity. Copywriter Neil French of the London Advertising Agency Holmes

Knight Ritchie wistfully opined of simpler advertising times "when the art of communication

was limited to press, posters, and TV – with radio if you knew a famous comedian to deliver the

script. Life was so much simpler" (Tungate, 2007, p. 100). Jenkins (2013) might have echoed

the practitioner's lament when she observed, in a more academic fashion, "convergence has

muddied the lines of demarcation surrounding media, technology, and culture" (p. 6).

Measurement tools and systems have not kept up with the complexities of media. Ultimately,

the current "proliferation of media has outstripped the means to measure cross-media

effectiveness" leaving marketers searching for alternatives (Assael, 2011, p. 1).

**Practitioner-scholar divide.** Meanwhile, the advertising industry is composed of two

branches from the same tree: practitioners and academics. While the two branches are as arms

literally joined at the torso, they often approach advertising from vastly different perspectives.

Royne (2012) asked, "How can researchers in the academic advertising arena contribute to the

advertising discipline as a whole?" (p. 544). The gap between practitioners and academics in the

field of advertising has been acknowledged and been the focus of scholarly study in itself

(Bogart, 1986; Hunt, 2002; Nyilasy & Reid, 2007; Nyilasy & Reid, 2009; Li, 2012). Nyilasy and

Reid (2012) describe the differing and sometimes competing views this way: "Practitioners have

to solve problems and act, while academicians reflect on reality and try to explain it" (p. 33).
The professional-scholar gap is a reality in the field that influences advertising research. Any realistic proposal for a cross-platform advertising delivery metric should attempt to be acceptable, indeed beneficial, to both those who practice advertising professionally and to those who study it academically.

There is a need to strengthen the relationship between advertising scholarship and practice. "Understanding practitioner opinions is important in that it provides an indication of the concerns and practices of the industry and potential future directions for academic research" (Cheong, Gregoria, & Kim, 2010, p. 405). As Rotfeld (2012) observed,

> For all the money spent on mass communications, [only] some of the more insightful practitioners see the value in the knowledge of a theoretical perspective that indicates whether something would work as expected or whether that money might be wasted. (p. 560)

In addition, as Lewin (1951) famously observed, "there is nothing so practical as a good theory" (p. 12). Clearly, any realistic scholarly approach to multimedia ad measurement must consider the needs of both the practitioner community as well as the academic community.

**Call for scholarship.** "One of the earliest pieces of advice given to most new researchers seeking to get their work published is to concentrate on filling in the gaps in the literature" (Kerr & Schultz, 2010, p. 547). Meanwhile, Matricon (1967) asserts:

> Advertising men have always wanted to know whether or not their ads have been read. At first, this was simply vanity on their part. But now that advertising is such a driving force in business, it is essential to know how many prospects have been reached and influenced by an advertising message. (p.33)

This calls to the forefront a crucial aspect of advertising measurement: message delivery.  Note that in the quote above, "reached" comes *before* "influenced."

Indeed, for decades, advertising practitioners and scholars have called for research on better measurement.  Stavitsky (2000) argued that new approaches to media ratings (delivery) research must be explored.  In particular, scholars urge advertising researchers to conduct qualitative investigations in instances in which literature reveals a need for rich and original data (Koslow, Sasser, & Riordan, 2003).  In addition, Cresswell (2012) recommended a qualitative methodology when a topic needs to be explored due to its immature nature or lack of theory.  Further, multiple researchers have called for empirical and qualitative academic research which integrates the perspectives of practitioners (Rossiter, 2001; Ottesen & Gronhaug, 2004; Nyilasy & Reid, 2007; Nyilasy & Reid, 2009).

Duff and Faber (2011) found it "interesting that virtually all the literature in advertising looks at what happens *after* [emphasis added] attention has been paid directly to the ad itself" (p. 51).  Of course, such research has value as it has composed the bulk of (non-creative) advertising study since before the field coalesced into a recognizable area of scholarship.  However, it is also important to investigate the actual delivery – that space between the sending of the message and its reception; in other words: *message delivery*.  Without knowledge and comparability metrics regarding delivery, it is arguable that study of so-called psychological effects is premature.

Separately, Laczniak (2015) suggested the current body of advertising research lacked strong theories which could contain "generalizations that could be made for all receivers, across all media, for all messages (e.g., exposure to ads will lead receivers to view brands in a more favorable manner)" (p. 431).  Perhaps a single measure of delivery across all media might open a path for broader perspectives to be applied across advertising.

Without question, one of the chief drivers of the cross-platform expansion is digital media growth. Cheong, Gregoria, and Kim (2010) encouraged researchers "to focus on developing new (and refining established) models that can better integrate the Internet's unique characteristics with more traditional media" (p. 414).

Cross-platform advertising delivery is based on data and data-driven research which "may be the best way for advertising academicians to contribute to the discipline" (Royne, 2012, p. 544). Therefore, a study of message delivery and advertising impressions might offer a beneficial contribution to both the academic discipline and practice of advertising.

**Dearth of delivery studies.** There is a relative lack of scholarly advertising studies that examine message delivery. Some of the shortfalls in delivery studies are likely because other topic areas might be considered more "sexy." As mentioned earlier, scholars have tended to focus on topic areas such as media effects, psychological processing (AKA persuasion and/or engagement), and creative/message design. In their zeal to delivery richer, more explanatory value, much academic advertising research has focused on "how" advertising works and far less on the nuts and bolts of delivery. There is even active discouragement for studies of message delivery. For example, Paine (2009) argues that traditional measures, such as impressions and "column inches" (p. 22) have become irrelevant. She argues that advertisers should track social media comments instead of just views or downloads. Other measurement concepts such as sales/revenue metrics, cost per point (CPP), as well as newly-created practitioner concepts such as the Brand Immersion Model (Steele et al., 2013) – which is the belief that characteristics of the media and goals of the viewer plus the interaction of the two have an impact on viewer experiences – and a host of others have been proposed. The present challenge to be addressed here is to develop and examine a single measure of delivery for advertising messages that can be applied across all media.

Another contributing factor to the low volume of delivery studies is that some scholars have staked out territory and argued for what they believe is important to the understanding of advertising and its influence. Such arguments often seem to assume that delivery will take place. This bias has a long history, and advertising practitioners have also contributed to it. In 1903, Powers – in an early example of advertising scholarship – discussed many factors regarding advertising. However, he offered no mention of delivery measurement.

In 1959, the National Industrial Conference Board conducted a survey of advertisers to determine the common areas of concern for advertising management (Patti, 1977). As a result of their survey, the Board initiated major studies dealing with the following topics:

1. evaluating spending strategies;

2. pretesting advertising;

3. evaluating media; and,

4. measuring advertising effectiveness (p. 30).

Notably, these priorities also omit message delivery. One might suppose that perhaps media delivery could exist somewhere between topic number 3 "evaluating media" and topic number 4 "measuring advertising effectiveness" – however, delivery is not specifically delineated. Simply put: delivery must be measured. After all, a major consideration, observed by Karlsson (2007), is that "not all messages get through" (p. 10). John Wanamaker, former US Postmaster General and department store magnate, famously declared, "I know half of my advertising is wasted, I just don't know which half" (Adage.com as cited in Luo & Donthu,

2001, p. 7). Rotfeld (2007) also argues that a significant amount of advertising money is wasted – perhaps as much as two thirds.

Further, Campbell (1965) offered 9 dependent variables for advertising results, which he suggests in "descending order of measurement desirability" (p.2): (1) Sales, (2) Market share, (3) Purchasers, (4) Distribution, (5) Momentum, (6) Attitude, (7) Knowledge, (8) Awareness, and (9) Playback. Yet Campbell also makes no mention of advertising delivery. Here again, it seems *assumed* that target audience members will be exposed to the advertisement. The critical component of delivery is often merely assumed (and thus neglected) in the extant literature.

Separately, Gibson (1983) claimed that the most important advertising-effectiveness measure is persuasion which links directly to sales. Subsequently, in a 30-year, multiple-journal, longitudinal analysis of advertising research featured in major marketing, communication, and advertising journals, Kim, Kayes, Avant, and Reid (2014) found that the most commonly studied topic areas were advertising practice, advertising effects, social issues, advertising-related effects, advertising content, and methodology. However, studies dealing with message delivery were virtually non-existent.

In summary, scholarly research on advertising has almost ignored advertising delivery as a topic. Most advertising performance measures focus on one of two areas: (1) the psychological processes within the minds of the consumers, including such concepts as engagement and persuasion, or (2) behavioral outcomes subsequent to advertising exposures, such as recall and/or purchasing behavior. It's important to call out that both of these 'effects' could only happen *after* a message was delivered. While these are important subjects, the literature does not meaningfully address the measurement of message delivery – and especially not on a cross-platform basis. How can marketers properly evaluate "effectiveness" if they do not have information on whether the message was actually delivered (or to what extent it may have been delivered) via the various media or channels they use?  How is it possible to evaluate media or adjust media mix without comparative measurement?  Most important, how can the industry begin to measure omni-channel advertising effectiveness without the crucial pre-cursor of a cross-platform delivery metric?  As the number of media vehicles expands and evolves, there is a growing need to look at the delivery of advertising messages across multiple media.  This study explores the potential of a single measure of delivery for all media: the impression.

**Conclusion**

This first chapter introduced the challenge, discussed the background and scope of the issue, made the case for the need for this research, and stated the specific purpose of this study.

The second chapter will be a review and discussion of literature relevant to the topic.

# Chapter 2

**How Advertising Got Us Here**

This chapter reviews literature relevant to this study by summarizing the scope of advertising research, providing a working definition of advertising, and including some historical perspective on the topic. Further, it presents the major theories used in advertising and observes the need for a cross-platform approach to advertising. Then two theoretical approaches and a conceptual model are suggested as possibilities for interpreting results from this study. Finally, this section ends with proposed research questions tied to the study's purpose which will guide and be addressed in the study overall.

**Advertising Research, Scope and Definition**

For an activity that is so prevalent and intertwined into American life as advertising, it is strange that the academic community has brought to bear no grand theories of advertising to unite the field. There are many theories applied to advertising, but they are generally borrowed from other fields. Nan and Faber (2004) refer to advertising as a variable field developed from the common interests of marketing and communication. Others assert that advertising borrows more from psychology, sociology, and even anthropology, as well as business, economics, and other fields of study (Thorson & Rodgers, 2012).

Above and beyond the business impact, advertising has attracted voluminous and sustained academic study for more than a century. In an early article from the *Annals of the American Academy of Political and Social Science*, Powers (1903) asked how and where businesses should advertise; he observed that advertising "involves the question of mediums and localities" (p. 473).  Since the 1920's, advertising researchers have essentially tried to address this question and studied advertising in many ways, some of it focused on determining the effectiveness of advertising initiatives.  There are at least seven academic journals dedicated specifically to advertising, including the *Journal of Advertising, Journal of Advertising Research, Journal of Advertising History*, and others.  Further, there are numerous marketing, business, and communication journals that regularly deal with the subject.

Despite this considerable tradition of academic advertising research, a clear and concise definition of the term "advertising" remains somewhat elusive and continues to evolve.  Definitions of advertising often include multiple components (creative, message, media, delivery, targeting, audience, impression, persuasion, sales, etc.).  Richards and Curran (2002) examined more than three dozen definitions and engaged a host of experts in a study using three waves of a Delphi panel to develop the definition used in the present study, "Advertising is a paid, mediated form of communication from an identifiable source, designed to persuade the receiver to take some action, now or in the future" (p. 74).  And the work continues: Reed and Ewing (2004) observed "despite more than a century of work in the area, numerous fundamental questions remain largely unanswered" (p. 92).

**Brief History of Advertising**

The earliest extant examples of advertising have been found among the first-century ruins of ancient Pompeii.  As newspapers began in the seventeenth century (France) and eighteenth century (England), advertising as we know it today began to take shape.  However, many histories of advertising do not begin until the nineteenth century (Tungate, 2007).

During the industrial revolution – with the widespread adoption of printing presses – newspapers (and advertising) took off.  From the 1700's through the early 1900's, newspapers were the dominant media. Consequently, newspaper advertising was the dominant form of advertising.  In 1922, as the medium of radio began to take hold in the United States, the first radio commercials were aired on WEAF in New York City (Advertising Age, 1999).  Polling research that would eventually become instrumental in advertising measurement got its modern start when George Gallup, while still an employee of the ad agency Young & Rubicam, started the American Institute of Public Opinion (which later became the Gallup Organization (Blackwell, n.d.; Tungate, 2007 ).  The first television commercials aired on WNBT (also in New York City) in 1941, ushering in the television advertising era (Advertising Age, 1999).  As the American media landscape continued to evolve, the advertising landscape has progressed right along with it.

Academically, advertising programs of study began to appear mostly in journalism schools, and eventually, many became part of communication majors.  Initially, the programs were mostly technical and trade-oriented as "research was absent from the earliest programs, but became a staple item starting after World War II" (Preston, 2012, p. 532).  Today advertising is studied in departments of business, marketing, and communication, as well as departments of psychology, sociology, and anthropology – and even a few departments of advertising.

**Theories Applied to Advertising**

Kim, Kayes, Avant, and Reid (2014) found that the most common theories applied to advertising study since 1980 were (1) dual-process models, including elaboration-likelihood, (2) involvement (AKA engagement), (3) information processing theory, (4) interactivity, and (5) source credibility.  The models that are used most are of the hierarchy approach.  Hierarchy of effects models assumes a cognition leads to an effect and subsequently to a behavior (Vakratsas

& Ambler, 1999).  These approaches focus on psychological aspects of advertising that, yet

again, can only begin *after* exposure to the message has occurred.

Integrated marketing communication (IMC), another concept and practice prominently

emphasized in recent scholarly literature, is also relevant to the current discussion.  The IMC

approach acknowledges that the lines between different marketing activities have begun to

overlap.  "IMC is a market-relating deployment mechanism that enables the optimization of

communication approaches to achieve superior communication effectiveness, which has other

downstream benefits (e.g., brand and financial performance)" (Luxton, Reid, & Mavondo, 2015,

p. 37).  Nowak and Phelps (1994) suggest three views of IMC, ranging from "one voice" to

"simultaneous objectives" to "coordinated marketing" (p. 51).  However, they also lament that

there is no measure for cross-media advertising expenditures.  Kitchen, Kim, and Schultz (2008)

cite another disconnect between practitioners and theorists regarding IMC: "in spite of the

continuing theoretical confusion, a large number of agencies and marketing organizations

continue to deploy 'integrated marketing' or 'integrated marketing communication'" programs

(p. 531).

Additionally, as advertising is mediated and the lines between media (also between major

media types, devices, social media platforms -- and applications related to them) are also

beginning to blur, many of the distinctions between advertising media have begun to melt away.

As such, IMC emphasizes the power of advertising across multiple media (Naik & Raman, 2003;

McGrath, 2005).  Yet, the delivery measures for advertising stubbornly remain differentiated by

*siloed* media.  Although IMC offers concepts that point in the right direction, it also fails to

suggest actual theories or applications that might offer a useful approach to the delivery

measurement conundrum.  Nonetheless, IMC scholars have called for additional research into the topic of measurement (Kitchen, Kim, & Schultz, 2008; Reinold & Tropp, 2012).  Specifically,

Schultz, Block, and Raman (2009) also called for cross-media comparison measures.

As noted previously, much advertising study has used hierarchy of effects models or

persuasion theories, such as McGuire's (1961) inoculation theory, Lavidge and Steiner's (2000)

hierarchy of advertising effects, and Petty and Cacioppo's (1984) elaboration likelihood model.

These theories all envision, more or less, a logical progression of mostly linear mental activity

leading to persuasion.  Inoculation theory suggests that resistance can be developed to an

argument, similar to the way that the body develops resistance to disease: by previous exposure,

thus interrupting the linear process.  Lavidge and Steiner "postulated a hierarchical sequence of

effects, resulting from the perception of an advertisement, which moves the consumer ever closer

to purchase" (Palda, 1966, p. 13).  The order is generally along the lines of attention (awareness),

interest, desire, and then action (AIDA) following Strong's (1925) observations.  One of the

most popular persuasion/advertising theories is the elaboration likelihood theory (ELT) of Petty

and Cacioppo (1984).  ELT is "a dual-process model for persuasion that describes two paths to

persuasion: the central, and the peripheral route" (Chmielewski, 2012, p. 35).  The central path is

used by a person when he or she is motivated and involved in the topic.  He or she looks for

information (elaborates) on the message and thinks through, or actively processes, information to

make a decision.  On the other hand, the peripheral route is the route used when a person does

not pay close attention to the persuasive communication and tends to make decisions on various

other cues, e.g., auto-pilot thinking.  Although widely used, there are criticisms of logical-

progression models.  For example, some argue that people don't necessarily think in a logical

order and sometimes skip steps that the models suggest.  Further, Johnson and Eagly (1990) have

questioned ELT's proposition that there are only two routes of information processing.  More generally, Palda (1966) has questioned the assumed link between attitude and behavior: Does attitude necessarily direct and/or precede behavior?

Even as the advertising field has evolved and as the media landscape has become more complex, a great deal of advertising research has remained over-focused on such theories of persuasion and attitude change (Nan & Faber, 2004; Faber, Duff, & Nan, 2012); however, for advertising theory to move forward, scholars must study concepts that are particular to the field of advertising itself – and especially those that have the potential to address the complex realities that face practitioners today. One area that is still in need of more research is delivery measurement.

Shen (2002) observed the need for consistent metrics across multiple media for advertisers to make "apple[s]-to-apple[s] comparisons with other media in campaign planning and evaluations" and further suggested the impression as a viable cross-media metric "because it is a traditional media term that is readily comparable to other media" (p. 59).

Danaher and Dagger (2013) conducted a cross-platform experiment in Australia to test the relative effectiveness of 10 media outlets. To implement their study, they realized the need for a single, comparable measure of advertising exposure but they created a concept of aggregate ratings from reported exposures instead of using the exposures themselves. The result was somewhat complex. A measure of effectiveness was not clearly delineated although purchase incidence and revenue from sales were used as representative measures. Finally, they used the combined data to arrive at a media optimization recommendation. Studies incorporating multiple metrics to attempt to quantify effectiveness are not surprising. As academics and practitioners alike struggle to find solutions to cross-platform advertising, they are aware that they lack the data and tools that are up to the challenge. Voorveld, Neijens, and Smit (2011) state that multimedia campaigns or cross-media campaigns are used by advertisers to optimize the "effectiveness of their budgets by exploiting the unique strengths of each medium" (p.69). Yet, there remains a disconnect between the desire to utilize cross-platform advertising and the capability of evaluating the practice. As Taylor et al. (2013) observed, marketers are deficient in the information they require to make intelligent media decisions in a complicated, multimedia environment. This furthers the argument for the need of a cross-platform metric.

**Advertising Impression Measurement**

Advertising can be measured from multiple perspectives and in different ways. For example, a cost-to-reach metric based on impressions is used for some advertising media. However, that impression-based approach is not often used to compare delivery across multiple media to a specific target. As presented in Chapter 1, this study proposes to explore that comparative delivery measure from five perspectives across the advertising industry, including advertising agencies; advertising media sellers; advertising clients; scholars who study advertising; and organizations/companies that report or advocate for advertising measurement.

Reaching consumers in the target audience(s) with a message is an important goal of media placement. Given that media budgets are limited, marketers or advertisers must be able to measure and report on the success and/or failure of their efforts. These objectives are often measured by two concepts used to provide a perspective on message delivery: reach and frequency. Reach is the number of unduplicated people (or percent) that are estimated to be exposed to the message; frequency is a measure of how many times the average person has seen the message (frequency includes duplication) (Danaher, 2007). However, these are usually estimates and involve averages derived from complex distribution formulas. The related concept of impressions is one element of the reach and frequency calculations. In *media math*, reach multiplied by frequency equals gross impressions.  An impression can also be thought of as a single exposure to a message.  One of the major criticisms of the reach and frequency approach is that it is only based on estimates using mathematical calculations of who might have seen/heard an advertising message an average number of times: most often through a version of a (beta) binomial distribution formula.  As a practical matter, reach and frequency are still widely used in media planning and buying, albeit (as noted earlier) usually in a siloed manner.

"For decades, advertising scholars have used Lasswell's (1948) 'Who says What in Which Channel to Whom with What Effects' as a framework to develop theories of how advertising works" (Gangadharbatla, 2012, p. 404) – and the basic premise still has utility in the modern media environment even though increasingly detailed concepts such as media planning and placement have evolved.  According to Tungate (2007), media strategy only became a developed area of thinking and practice as recently as the 1990s (pp.7-8).  But, despite common practitioner usage, there is a dearth of impression-based scholarly research.  However, Elsen, Pieters, and Wedel (2016) have studied "thin slice impressions" (p. 567) or exposures of a very short duration, for example, less than a few seconds.  And impressions still matter to the practitioner community.  Canoe, a joint venture of leading cable television companies, is a leading supplier of video-on-demand advertising.  Canoe served up ads delivering more than 11 billion impressions in 2015 – representing a 75% growth from the previous year.  This type of new media does not conform to any existing media measurements; however, impressions represent a useful construct for inclusion of this medium.  Further, Jacobowitz (personal communication, October 28, 2016) of Spectrum Reach is studying impressions based on cable set top box (STB) data.

Advertising measurement is a broad concept indeed.  As indicated above, there are numerous advertising measurements that have been used over the past century or so.  The present

challenge is to explore a single measure of delivery for advertising messages that can be applied

across all media.  The impression offers potential to address that need.


**Syndicated Measurement & Major Providers**

The 2013 merger of Nielsen and Arbitron, along with the 2016 merger of Comscore and

Rentrak, left two players dominating the electronic syndicated media measurement industry;

Nielsen controls approximately 80% of the market while Comscore has almost 20% (Martin &

Medina, 2015).  Both companies appear to be angling to be the leading providers of cross-

platform media measurement as they attempt to clean up advertising's "massive measurement

mess" (Lafayette, 2015, p. 6).  Mostly, these leading audience measurement companies measure

media exposures.  Nielsen, which has long measured television, now has Arbitron's radio

business, along with its own online measurement properties.  Its measurement is mostly panel- or

sample-based, primarily utilizing approximately 20,000 people meters attached to home

televisions and portable people meters (PPM) for measuring radio.

To its leading Internet measurement services, Comscore adds Rentrak's motion picture

services as well as Rentrak's set top box television measurement.  Different from Nielsen,

Comscore focuses primarily on census-based measurement – capturing all ad clicks or all

viewing from set top boxes.  Rentrak is now advocating for a so-called basket of currencies or

complementary measurement tools to purport to measure cross-platform media delivery while

Nielsen seems to be trying to 'go it alone.'  So, it seems that the major measurement companies

are taking steps to move toward a more inclusive cross-platform metrics.  As the primary

providers of audience measurement data, Lafayette (2016) argues that third-party arbiters help provide cross-media comparability and that they are the "only ones who can determine unduplicated reach across multiplatform campaigns" (p. 28).

Webster and Ksiazek (2012) utilized Nielsen's TV/Internet Convergence Panel to develop an audience-centric approach to fragmentation. The TV/Internet Convergence Panel has a sample of about 1,000 homes that strives to maintain sample membership over time. But, the panel tracks just two media: television and computer-based Internet (not mobile). In October 2016, Nielsen announced it was bringing to market an out-of-home measurement solution that makes use of Arbitron's Portable People Meter technology to measure television viewing in bars, restaurants, and other out-of-home locations. Nielsen has also created a social media measurement arm (NM Incite) and Nielsen Twitter TV Ratings (NTTR) that reports "tweet volume and tweet impressions" for programs (van Es, van Geenen, & Boeschoten, 2016, para. 5).

Though the TV/Internet Panel and Twitter ratings can (just barely) be considered cross-platform (with two media), the out-of-home measurement effort and the social media project still measure just a single platform each. Although Nielsen, Comscore, and others have been giving lip service to cross-platform metrics for years, today there remain few if any viable options for holistic cross-platform measurement.

There do not appear to be any meta-analyses of cross-platform media measurement; although this would be an excellent topic for future research. Minimal scholarly research has been conducted on Comscore or Rentrak, although one study used Comscore data (Yunjae, Leckenby, & Eakin, 2011) to compare magazine and Internet exposures. A few studies looked at Arbitron in the context of topics such as listener loyalty (Dick & Mcdowell, 2004) and portable people meters (Tudor, 2009), but none studied advertising – although the Tudor study did look at cross-platform on a limited basis by analyzing media exposure across both TV and radio.

Meanwhile, Nielsen was the lone major research vendor that received more significant academic

attention. Recent studies featuring Nielsen focused on the history and evolution of television

ratings (Buzzard, 2015), Politics (Kernell & Rice, 2011; Jomini Stroud, Stephens & Pye, 2011),

demographics of television show cast members (Shachar & Emerson, 2000), and local TV news

(McDowell, 2008). Again, none of the studies featuring Nielsen dealt with cross-platform

exposure, and none looked at multiple media.

**Impression & Cross-Platform**

Any viable metric for advertising delivery must possess two simultaneous properties: (1)

The potential to be broadly applied across multiple media platforms, and (2) The ability to

account for individual exposures at a specific, individual level.

The impression meets these criteria. As a cross-platform measure, it has several benefits,

including its elegant parsimony. The impression is uniquely suited to address what Smit and

Neijens (2011) state are essential advertising questions: "Audience research tries to answer

questions such as, 'How many people were exposed to my advertisement?' and 'How often were

they exposed?'" (p. 124). Traditional reach and frequency do provide calculated estimates to try

to answer these questions. However, in practice, the calculations are media-dependent and

virtually impossible to apply across multiple media.

Further, the basic currency in media planning is the number of people reached by an

advertising message carried by a particular media vehicle. Advertising exposures, (also called

impressions) are "generally considered to be the most valid indicator for reach;" meanwhile,

socio-psychological factors "such as persuasion and behavioral responses are not considered as

valid because these are affected by factors beyond the control of the media, such as the attractiveness of the advertised product or service and the power of copy and artwork" (Smit &

Neijens, 2011, p. 125).

In other words, media vehicle representatives (sellers) might argue that they did their job

(delivered the message to the target audience), but if the message itself is bad or the product is

not in demand, then those are not problems with advertising or message delivery. It is critical to

measure message delivery earlier in the process than attempt to measure attitude change because

exposure is a necessary pre-cursor for message effect. With all advertising, "a fundamental

concept is that the consumer/viewer must first be exposed before any communication or

persuasion can occur. Thus, ability to capture attention and [to] sustain interest have become

important research measures" (Gruber, 1966, p. 14).

According to Wang (2006), engagement is a measure of contextual relevance impacting

the brand that influences recall, involvement, believability, and attitude (p. 355). But the so-

called socio-psychological factors popular with scholars (and some practitioners) are difficult,

time-consuming, and expensive to measure. As such, they are often impractical to scale for all

but the largest companies. Further, such measures of individual perception/effect, while useful

in developing advertising content, do not address delivery of the message in scaled media

placement.

Pergelova, Prior, and Rialp (2010) observed that advertising effects on sales may play out

over months or years. Time frames like that are far too long for advertising delivery needs. Kerr

and Schultz (2010) assert that the academic advertising research model is simply "broken or

badly outdated" (p. 547). They argue that the academic community has failed to keep up with

the need in the industry: "The enormity of change in advertising compounded by the lack of

response from researchers suggests the traditional academic advertising research model requires more than routine maintenance" (p. 547).  Arguably, the tools and concepts of the past simply do not meet the cross-platform challenges of today.

Meanwhile, the popular paradigm of integrated marketing communication (IMC) does focus attention on cross-platform, multi-media messaging, and the measurement of related aspects of the implementation of that approach.  "IMC has made message delivery, and consequently media choice, far more important in the messaging process" (Rose, 2012, p. 564).

From the practitioner perspective, scholars may already be latent in acknowledging the impression-based approach to omni-channel advertising.  Brock Thompson, Los Angeles-based VP of Local Ad Sales for Time Warner Cable Media, Los Angeles, observed: "An impression is an impression is an impression – whether it's seen on TV or whether it is seen on a tablet or whether it's seen on your iPhone" (Salescast, 2015).

Some scholars have argued that advertising research must evolve away from an intra-media approach to an inter- or cross-media approach (Assael, 2011; Jessen & Graakjær, 2013).  And as media evolve, the formats may become less distinct due to the technological tools used to access different media (AKA devices).  Thus, Varan et al. (2013) and Thorson and Rodgers (2012) importantly noted that it is critical to measure across not just media formats, but also across devices.  Pergelova, Prior, and Rialp (2010) noted that "an important issue for advertisers is how to integrate different media and messages in order to produce a desired effect (brand image, sales, etc.)" (p. 49).  But before the 'desired effect' can be measured, advertisers must have the ability to compare the *delivery* of their messages across that plethora of media options.

The AdImpact method is an example of a tool developed to compare exposure to different media utilizing impressions; the proportion of total money going into each medium for a defined product field is made equivalent to the total exposure units for that medium (Corder,

1986).  While that particular model is more appropriate for a financial analysis, it lends credence to the impression as a cross-platform metric.

Further, the all-important Internet as an advertising medium is following some of the legacy media in adopting impressions as a measurement metric.  Shen (2002) suggested that web advertising follow the "exposure-based model" in which advertisers pay for "impressions or opportunities to see, much like they pay for ads on television and in other media" (p. 61).  Huang and Lin (2006) have also studied the impression for use in planning for Internet advertising.  Meanwhile, Learmonth (2010) discussed Google's ad impression delivery measurement.  In addition, Danaher, Lee, and Kerbache (2010) utilized impressions to develop an Internet advertising optimization model.  More recently, Flosi, Fulgoni, and Vollman (2013) observed that "the primary metric used to buy and sell online advertising" is still the impression (p. 192).

In general, as advertisers and marketers continue to invest more heavily in online advertising in addition to varied legacy media, they are demanding a delivery metric that works across multiple media.  So, there is a need for cross-platform measurement, and the impression may be a viable option to explore.  The following section discusses perspectives, including general systems theory, which may be helpful in evaluating the impression for multi-media advertising delivery.

**General Systems Theory**

Although there is not a theory that aligns perfectly with impression measurement, there is a meta-theoretical perspective that can offer a valuable framework from which to begin: general systems theory.

According to Laszlo (1972), systems theory approaches are widely applied to natural, social, and human sciences.  A general systems theory perspective, advocated by Von

Bertalanffy (1972), offers significant potential for studying complex systems and processes such as advertising.  Originally referred to as 'organismic biology,' general systems theory (GST) is a meta-theoretical approach to investigation that applies the analogy of a biological system to organizations and processes.  Systems theory offers a perspective that argues for the interrelatedness of concepts organized in a hierarchy of subsystems and supersystems (Smallwood, 1992).  GST places great importance on both process and flow while considering relationships among and between parts of the system to each other and their environments (inter-connectedness).  Von Bertalanffy (1972) promoted the concept of open systems models – those that have exchanges with the world external to the systems themselves.  Systems have three primary structural components: inputs, throughputs (AKA transformations), and outputs.  Further, systems may also include smaller "subsystems" or be part of larger "supersystems" (aka "suprasystems.")  By definition, systems have boundaries that separate them from their environments; in other words, there are things – concepts, elements, etc. – that are inside the system as well as those that are outside a given system.  The elements of a system work together to yield a sum that is greater than its parts.  Another important element of GST is the principle of equifinality, which states that systems can reach the same end state from different beginning conditions and via different routes (Katz & Kahn, 1978).  GST offers an appropriate lens to examine processes such as advertising.  More than forty years ago, Kast and Rosenzweig observed that "a vast literature in modern organization theory…has explicitly or implicitly adopted systems theory as a frame of reference" (1972, p.451).  Multiple theorists have applied systems theory to the study of organizations and organizational communication (Barnard, 1938; March & Simon, 1958; Farace, Monge, & Russell, 1977; Katz & Kahn, 1978; Cummings, Long, & Lewis, 1987; Hazleton, 1992; Smallwood, 1992; Leischow & Milstein, 2006; and Colapinto &

Porlezza, 2012).  As there has been a significant volume of organizational research conducted from a systems perspective, there is theoretical justification for the use of GST in the study of the organizational communication activity of advertising.

Advertising and public relations can both be considered part of the larger concept of marketing.  The so-called four P's of marketing: price, place, product, and promotion -- place advertising together with public relations into the category of promotion thus linking them closely together (Thorson & Rodgers, 2012).  An example of how the meta-theoretical perspective of GST has been used in a field under the marketing umbrella and closely related to advertising is the public relations process model of Long and Hazleton (1987).  This particular application of GST may offer explanatory value for the present study.

**The Public relations process model.**  The public relations process model of Long and Hazleton (1987) proposes a theoretic and practical description and definition of public relations from a general systems theory approach.  (See Figure 1.)  They define public relations as "a communication function of management through which organizations adapt to, alter, or maintain their environment for the purpose of achieving organizational goals" (p. 6).  They consider quantitative and qualitative aspects of public relations behavior and permit analysis within and across subsystems or between subsystems and the environment.

The PR process model is based on an open systems model that envisions an over-arching environmental supersystem with three subsystems.  The environmental supersystem provides exogenous input into the three subsystems. These external inputs further affect endogenous inputs within each subsystem.  Exogenous inputs into the PR system are complex, consisting of five interrelated, interacting dimensions (see below).  Meanwhile, the entire model -- and each subsystem -- contains an input, transformation, output cycle.

The three subsystems each contain important elements:

1.  Organizational Subsystem – The first subsystem contains organizational and public

    relations goals, resources, and strategy.

2.  Communication Subsystem – The second or middle subsystem contains the processes

    of message encoding and delivery.

3.  Target Audience Subsystem – Finally, the third subsystem contains the concepts of

    influence and/or maintenance/change of cognition/behavior.

**Figure 1**

*Public Relations Process Model*

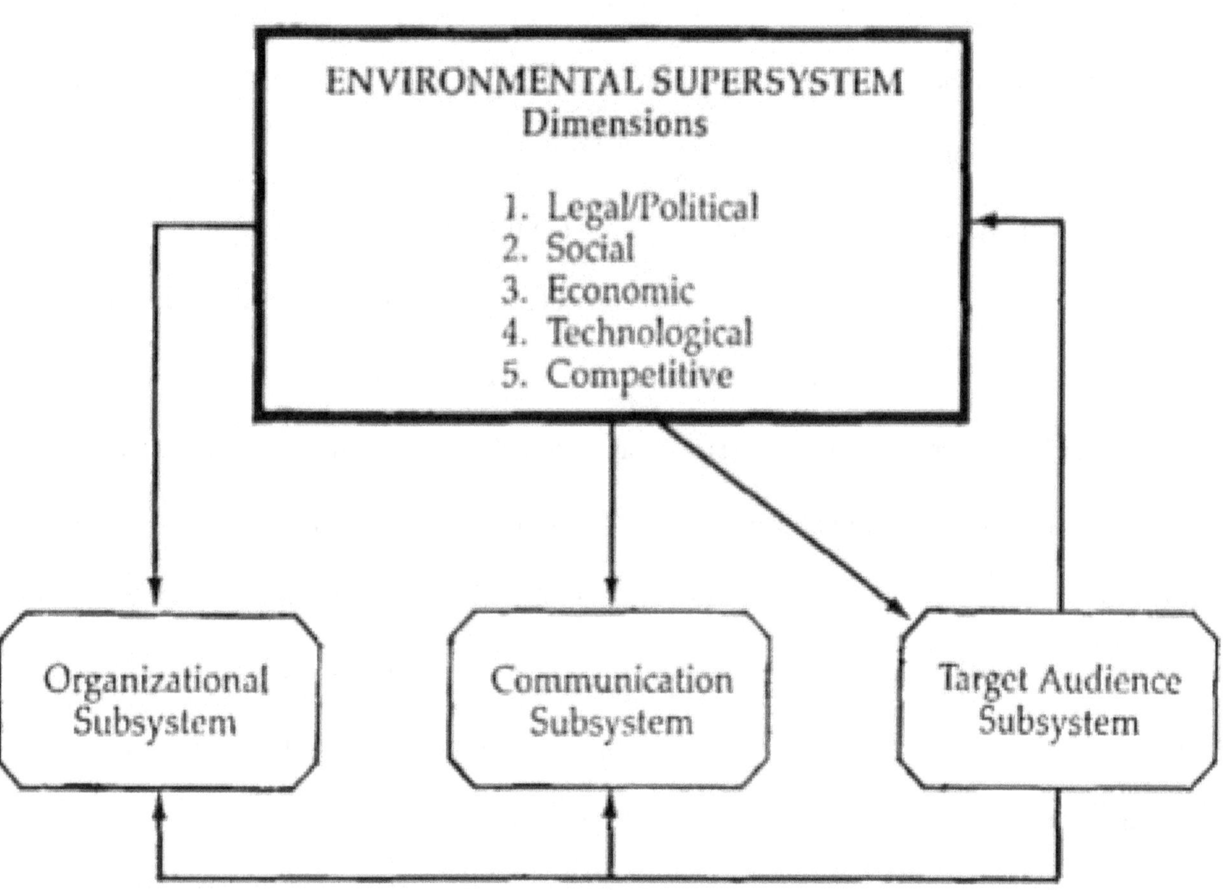

Further, the model includes five overlapping, interacting dimensions of the environment from the supersystem:

- Political/legal – This dimension is characterized by rules which govern organizational conduct and enforcement, including legislation and judicial processes.

- Economic – This dimension includes financial and monetary resources and constraints.

- Competitive – The competitive dimension includes an array of competitors, both internal to, and external to the industry.

- Technological – This dimension includes technology, devices, and/or knowledge systems (software) impacting the organization.

- Social – Finally, the social dimension includes the public and stakeholders of the organization.

The PR process model is a theoretical approach that specifically recognizes message delivery. It does so within the communication subsystem. The outputs of the communication subsystem are messages to which audiences may be exposed. "Physically, messages are tangible stimuli that can be perceived" (Long & Hazleton, 1987, p. 11). It is the actual perception of the message, measurement of the delivery, and how it is reported that are of most relevance to the present study. The PR process model provides an applicable framework from which to understand message delivery better. While the present study is intended to solicit input from industry leaders, a GST perspective, informed by the PR process model, may prove helpful in providing an analytical context for organizing and evaluating the results.

What's missing from both academia and practice is a single method to quantify delivery and compare cost-to-benefit ratios of advertising delivery on a multi-platform basis. Without such a tool, advertising practitioners and scholars will continue to try to create comparisons that are essentially like trying to compare fractions without a common denominator. The use of the impression as a common metric across all media might offer a path forward to fill this gap.

**Conceptual Justification for Sampling Strata**

Thorson and Rodgers (2012) proposed several elements as part of the advertising process, including three primary components: advertising organizations (agencies), message sources (advertisers), and channels (media). From the practitioner perspective, there is also a need to include measurement vendors and advocacy organizations -- which are playing a leading role in developing advertising measurement (Gladys Yu, March 16, 2016, personal communication & Jason Darwin, April 5, 2016, personal communication). Further, to help cross the practitioner-scholar divide, including the perspectives of advertising and communication scholars may yield additional insights. Therefore, the present study proposes such a path forward by soliciting evaluative viewpoints along that path from all sides of the advertising industry – calling on the five key groups outlined above to help offer a holistic perspective for the overall advertising community, particularly as it relates to advertising measures of cross-platform delivery and opportunities:

1. advertising buyers (agencies)
2. advertising sellers  (media)
3. advertising clients (advertisers)
4. advertising measurement companies/advocate organizations (vendors)
5. academia (scholars who study advertising)

**Research Questions**

For reasons proposed herein and emerging from the foregoing evidence and literature review, this study seeks to address the following research questions:

Research Question 1: How do advertising professionals view advantages and disadvantages of the impression (CPM) as a single-measure of cross-platform message delivery?

RQ1 seeks to determine if there is a viable case to be made for the impression as a cross-platform media measurement from perspectives across the advertising community.

Research Question 2: What are the challenges in creating, implementing, and adopting an impression-based measurement approach for multiple advertising media?

RQ2 attempts to understand the obstacles that might hinder the implementation and adoption of the impression as a single measure of advertising delivery better.

Research Question 3: What additional considerations will need to be addressed regarding media measurement considering the dynamic media environment?

RQ3 explores what advertising industry experts believe are trends and issues pertaining to the current and future advertising and media environment which will have a bearing on measures of advertising effectiveness, especially as they relate to the prospect of a holistic, impression-based metric. Systemic factors in the industry, including professional roles, media proliferation, and the advertising process will be addressed.

Research Question 4: What are commonalities and differences among practitioners and academics regarding the topic of a single media delivery measurement and its implementation?

As indicated earlier, one tenet of this study is to include and investigate practitioner perspectives in addition to academic perspectives on advertising – specifically in regard to the potential of an advertising impression measurement approach. RQ4 examines the commonalities and/or differences between the two groups regarding the impression as a single, cross-platform message delivery metric.

**Conclusion**

This second chapter offered a review of relevant literature, a definition of advertising, and a brief historical perspective on advertising.  It also reviewed major theories used in advertising and commented on the need for a cross-platform approach.  The theoretic approach general systems theory was proposed, along with a specific application of GST, to provide a potential interpretative and analytical framework for this study.  Finally, this section proposed four research questions.

The third chapter presents the research design and methodology for this study.

# Chapter 3

**Research Design and Methodology**

This chapter discusses the design of the study, including the participants, and how the

sample was operationalized.  It also presents the interview approach and questioning rationale

along with the process used for the analysis.  This section ends with a brief discussion of

reflexivity.

**Design**

This study utilized a qualitative approach to examine current and potential delivery

metrics for major advertising-supported media from the academic and popular literature.  It

narrowed the focus to measurement of impression delivery as a single metric that may allow

comparability of various media vehicles (both content and device).  The study solicited opinions

from a variety of industry practitioners, as well as scholars, in the form of personal interviews.

Finally, these perspectives were integrated into an evaluation of the advertising impression

measurement (AIM) approach for advertising delivery, culminating in a proposed advertising

process model.

The primary goal was to understand the thinking of both advertising practitioners and

scholars from their perspectives and then to evaluate those thoughts relative to each other and in

the context of existing concepts of how advertising works; therefore, a qualitative design was

selected for the inquiry (Babbie, 1986; Creswell, 2009).  Two over-arching theoretical lenses are

brought to bear for interpretation.  First, although there is not an existing theoretical perspective

that fits perfectly, general systems theory offers an approach that may have value as a meta-theoretical framework.  The specific application of GST that most closely fits the needs of the current study is the public relations process model of Long and Hazleton (1987).  However, this approach lacked sufficient detail to capture and contextualize the findings and, therefore, needed further supplementation to incorporate greater granularity of detail.  As such, the study included supplemental qualitative analyses to begin to develop an advertising impression measurement (AIM) framework.  This approach was particularly useful in informing the study by helping to shape the data being explored as well as by providing interpretive lenses for the results.

**Participants**

The sample represented the five identified strata:

1. Buyers (Advertising Agencies)

2. Sellers (Media & Representation Firms)

3. Clients (Advertisers)

4. Research Vendors (Data, Measurement firm, or Advocacy Groups)

5. Academics (Scholars)

The goal was to obtain five to seven participants from each of these subgroups and to facilitate comparisons across the groups, as well as, synthesize a more holistic representation for the larger advertising community.  As part of the effort to include a representative mix from across the industry, one objective was to achieve a mix of gender participation.  Preference was given to participants who have at least 5 years' experience in the field of advertising, as well as those working with multiple media.  An additional preference was given to advertising clients with expenditures of more than $1 million per year on advertising utilizing multiple media. Participants were screened to meet these minimums and were also asked about their knowledge and experience in media measurement.  Screening questions included the length of time in current role and experience dealing with media measurement in the positions for the strata they represented.

Further, as recommended by Cresswell (2009), an interview protocol was followed. The specific protocol included header information (date, participants, etc.), interviewer instructions (so that the same procedures were followed for each interview), the planned interview questions, and probes for exploring some of the preplanned questions more fully, as well as a concluding statement of appreciation (Tuggle, 2014). This study used the qualitative technique of personal interviews with a small number of open-ended questions which Cresswell (2009) argued can successfully allow participants to share their experiences. The interview protocol and guide helped create both standardization (for similar experiences among participants) and flexibility (to enable the study to gain as much relevant information as possible).

**Sample.** Participants were selected from the five key areas indicated above across the advertising industry using the snowball method to fulfill a stratified, purposeful sample. This method aligns with recommendations by Coyne (1997) and Goulding (2005). In fact, intentional sampling is considered to be de rigeur for qualitative research. Actually, what Patton (2002) calls "purposeful" or "purposive" sampling is the "intended focus in qualitative sampling, and therefore a strength" (p. 230). A snowball sample was utilized beginning with industry contacts that the study author has built through 25 years in the advertising industry. Personal contacts were asked to identify additional potential participants and those participants, in turn, were asked to recommend other participants to fulfill sample goals.

Sample sizes are not often justified in qualitative research (Barnett, Vasileiou, Thorpe, & Young, 2015). According to Patton (2002), there are no hard and fast rules for sample size in qualitative inquiry. Mason (2010) argued that qualitative sample size should be enough to attain *saturation* – or that point at which no new concepts or significant ideas are added.  Guest, Bunce, and Johnston (2006) found that saturation often occurred around 12 interviews.  However, saturation can be difficult to pinpoint and is somewhat subjective.  Further, as a practical matter, operationalization of a research study can be difficult without some level of data-gathering goals.  In addition, Cresswell (2012) suggested 20-30 interviews for qualitative studies may be sufficient.  In keeping with the need to obtain sufficient representation from each of the strata, this study tried to satisfy both the saturation requirement and the recommendation above.  Therefore, the goal was to interview at least 30 participants distributed across the strata.

**Interviews**

Semi-structured, in-depth interviews were used as the key method of field inquiry.  Personal interviewing is an appropriate method for gathering rich, qualitative data (Creswell 2012).  Part of the difficulty in understanding the academician–practitioner gap has been the lack of true representation of the perspective of advertising practitioners within scholarly research.  Therefore, this study addressed that concern by including a variety of practitioners.  In-depth interviews allowed the discovery of perspectives from the participants.  Indeed, Baehr (2005) argued that interviewing may be one of the best methods of gathering data with the fewest inherent problems.  Each interview was planned for approximately 60-90 minutes.  Face-to-face interviews were the preferred format.  However, participants were drawn from major advertising locations across the U.S., including New York and Los Angeles.  Due to logistical concerns (costs and timeframe) of meeting with a wide variety of individual participants across a broad geography, a priority was given to getting access to participants wherever they were located.  Therefore, telephone and/or Skype/webcam were used on an as-needed basis – actually more often than face-to-face interviews.  The interviews were recorded and transcribed; detailed interview notes/field notes were also taken.  Each participant was offered confidentiality and permission to use each participant's information was secured.  Each participant was also invited to complete a participant background questionnaire.

The interview guide (Appendix A) was composed of nine questions derived from the four research questions.  The first two questions (#1 & #2) dealt with the participants' background in the industry and perceptions of current delivery measures.  The next three questions (#3, #4, & #5) related to the participants' thoughts on the impression as a cross-platform metric and challenges to implementing such a measure.  The following two questions (#6 & #7) dealt with additional participant considerations and their opinions on the evolution of measurement.  While the intent is to ask each sub-group the same questions to enhance comparison across the sub-groups, it was expected that each sub-group would likely bring different, valuable perspectives to the questions.  Prompts invited participants to share their unique perspectives for their sub-group.  Therefore, in addition, the participants were asked (#8) how they thought their perspectives might align with – or conflict with – those of others in the advertising community.  The final question (#9) was a query regarding additional concerns not specifically suggested by the interviewer that the participants thought might be relevant to the discussion.

**Reference Key**

For reference purposes in the discussion, participants are referenced using a key of lastname-strata.  The strata were Agency/Buyers = A; Media/Sellers = M; Advertisers/Clients = C; Researchers/Advocates = R; and Academics/Scholars = S.  For example, a media buyer from an advertising agency who is named Smith would be referred to as Smith (A).  This format helped to identify the group which each participant represented quickly.

**Analysis**

According to Corbin and Strauss (1990), it is important to note that data collection and analysis can be interrelated procedures. Also, the comments of the participants are the basic unit of analysis. Finally, the concepts were grouped and created into categories based on their relationships. In the case of this study, the analysis followed the coding of data recommended by grounded theory via three successive steps: 1) open coding, 2) axial coding, and 3) selective coding (Corbin & Strauss, 1990; Blythe, 2006; and Nyilasy & Reid, 2009) to develop categories based on the interview data. These three stages do not have to be performed in a linear fashion, but it may be helpful to consider them as such for explanatory reasons. Open coding is when the data sets are initially analyzed into convergent and divergent categories, and those categories are labeled using continuous comparisons. Axial coding is the next phase, and it is here that the categories are re-examined at a deeper level regarding sub-categories, continuously testing against the data as further development and refinement occurs. Third, in selective coding, the various categories that have emerged are attempted to be centralized around a "core" category, and descriptive detail is added to the categories as necessary. In this final section of coding, the researcher attempted to articulate the primary, over-arching findings of the data. The author coded, in the successive steps defined above, the concepts and articulations from the participants. Results were interpreted for the sub-groups and also collectively for the entire sample. Further, the results have been presented in the context of the GST-based public relations process model. Additional interpretive analysis was also developed through supplemental qualitative analyses based on additional stages of coding.

As the data is being evaluated, an "interplay between the empirical and conceptual realms, a novel perspective of the phenomenon being investigated is constructed" (Hirschman &

Thompson, 1997, p 46).  However, it is important that the developing relationships and theoretic constructs remain wholly supported by the observable and reported data.  Subsequent to the multi-level coding, the categories and relationships were described in detail.  Further, observed themes and patterns were identified and discussed.  According to Patton (2002), it is important to categorize, describe and theorize, taking steps to separate these efforts.

**Reflexivity and credibility.**  Concerns about reflexivity are especially cogent in the context of qualitative studies.  According to Patton (2002), "reflexivity reminds the qualitative inquirer to be attentive to and conscious of the cultural, political, social, linguistic, and ideological origins of one's own perspective and voice as well as the perspective and voices of those one interviews" (p. 65).  The study author, like all researchers, had a specific background, culture, and worldview that will be acknowledged and 'owned.'  Disclosure of factors that might affect the analysis is an important element in establishing credibility and allowing readers to understand potential biases.  There are three specific areas of self-reflexivity for which disclosure seems appropriate in this instance.  First, the author had prior business relationships with approximately one-third of the participants.  I have no reason to believe that the relationships had any negative impact on the input of the participants although that possibility exists.  However, I would argue that the relationships were beneficial to the study in that 1) my knowledge of the participants enhanced their fitness for the study, and 2) existing relationships made the conversations more comfortable for the participants.  Second, I have a bias that is a belief in the importance of measurement.  I did not share that belief with the participants and attempted to remain neutral when asking questions related to that topic.  However, there is the possibility that my opinions may have affected the analysis.  Patton (2002) observed that reflexivity is particularly relevant in terms of its impact on analysis and reporting.  Third, I am a native

English speaker with a southern accent. Several of the study participants were not native English speakers, and they had different accents which could have led to minor misunderstandings. I made every effort to speak clearly, repeat if necessary, and ask for clarification if I did not understand any of the participant responses.

Enhanced credibility was achieved through five methods: data triangulation, expert review, analytical triangulation, rigorous procedures, and multi-layered examinations and coding of the data. The first method of enhancing credibility was the triangulation of multiple qualitative data sources – 37 interviewees representing five different segments of the advertising industry were interviewed for the study. A second credibility factor was an expert review (operationalized through study author's 25 years of experience in the advertising industry). For example, little if any explanation of terms and concepts was necessary as the researcher and the study participants all had a firm grasp of the topics and language used in the field of advertising. Third, analytical triangulation was enabled by participant review – multiple participants were asked to review comments, quotes, and observations to ensure accuracy and reliability of interpretation. Fourth, consistent, rigorous procedures were followed by the same researcher for all interviews, thus maintaining consistency of questions, interview style, follow-up questions, and overall tone. Fifth and finally, specific attention was paid to minimizing what Patton (2002) calls the qualitative equivalent of statistical Type I (false positive) error. All observations were verified and confirmed with the data, usually requiring multiple observations and repetition of ideas and comments. The data itself (more than 900 pages of transcribed interviews) was reviewed no less than 20 times.

**Conclusion**

This third chapter reviewed the design of the study, including the participants, and how the sample was operationalized.  It also presented the interview approach and questioning

rationale along with the process used for the analysis and ended with notes on reflexivity and

credibility.

The fourth chapter presents the research findings for this study.

# Chapter 4

**Research Findings**

This chapter reviews the approach of the study, describes the sample, discusses the sample segmentation, outlines the participant organizational relevance to the topic based on financial expenditures (associated billing and/or revenue), and finally presents the findings for each research question, including emergent categorization of the data.

**Study Approach**

The purpose of this study was to examine perspectives across the advertising ecosystem in regard to the need for, nature of, and potential effectiveness of a cross-platform measure of advertising delivery – specifically the impression – through the lens of the systems-theory based public relations process model.  A qualitative research approach was used to solicit the opinions of diverse experts from the field of practice and academia about their past and current experiences with existing advertising measurement systems and tools; their ideas about what should be considered when developing an effective holistic industry metric suitable for the current and future advertising and digital media environment; and their insights about other trends that may influence the ways measures of advertising are created and used.  The goal was to integrate the opinions of these experts to evaluate a system of advertising measurement that addresses the need for consideration of how well advertising has been delivered – in the context of advertising efforts that are increasingly multi-media platform in character – when attempting to reach target markets or audiences who increasingly make use of many different forms of media and devices.  According to Patton (2002), with qualitative scholarship, "what people actually say and the descriptions of events observed remain the essence of qualitative inquiry" (p. 457).  With that guidance in mind, the findings and analysis for this study will contain a significant volume of direct quotes and observations.

**Study Participants**

Thirty-seven advertising professionals participated in the study spread across the five identified strata.  There were 13 females and 24 males; each of the five groups contained at least two females.

**Figure 2**

*Study Participants by Strata*

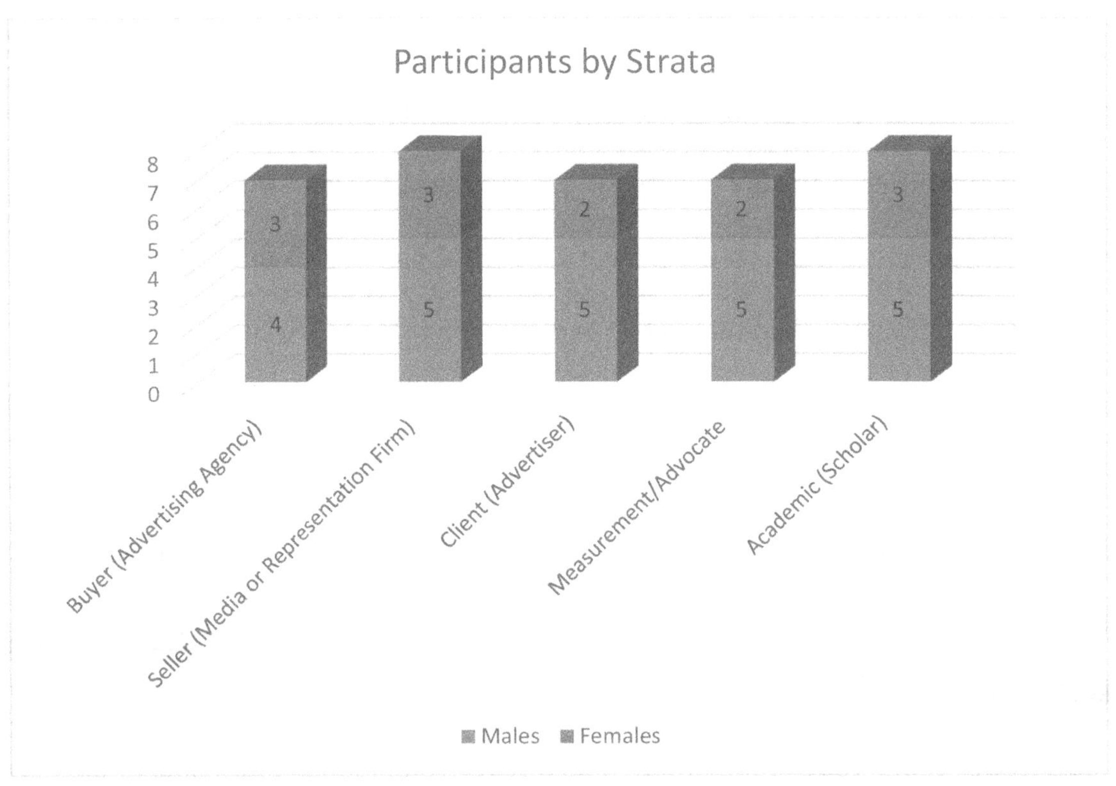


It is important to note that the opinions of the participants were theirs alone and not necessarily representative of the organizations and/or companies for which they are currently/were previously employed.  However, as the participants worked for some of the major advertising players in the United States – including Bank of America, Dr Pepper/Snapple, Nielsen, Group M, Turner Networks, Starcom, Facebook, Charter Communications, Domino's, Yahoo, and others – they bring a high level of credibility to this study.  Collectively, the participants and the organizations they represent accounted for as much as 20% of advertising spending, billing, and measurement worldwide.  Other participants represented esteemed industry organizations, such as the Media Ratings Council and the Interactive Advertising Bureau; these participants were key in that they provided a relatively unbiased perspective across multiple client groups and media platforms.  The academic participants included some of the most respected and broadly published scholars in the field of advertising.  The opinions of these professionals who work in, and study, the field of advertising were the primary units of analysis. A list of the participants (grouped by strata) appears in Table 1 below.  Also included were the names of the organization(s) with which each participant had a significant amount of experience. Most of them still worked at these organizations.  Note that the average professional experience (or academic study) in advertising for the participants was in excess of 10 years.  Virtually all served in fairly senior roles.  Educationally, all the participants had at least bachelor's degrees. Many held master's degrees, and two (beyond the scholars) also had Ph.D.s.  Interestingly, only a small handful (about 10%) of the 37 participants actually studied advertising or communication prior to entering the field.

**Segmentation (Strata Crossover)**

The five strata provide an important method of segmenting the sample and, collectively, the different groups brought a valuable variety of perspectives to the topic at hand.  This segmentation also provided a useful analytical component to the study.  However, it must be acknowledged that the strata were not completely discrete.  It was discovered that many of the

**Table 1**

*Study Participants by Strata/Organization*

**Buyer (Advertising Agency)**

| | | | |
|---|---|---|---|
| 1. | Debbie | Basham | MediaHub |
| 2. | Richard | Fielding | Starcom / Kantar |
| 3. | George | Mafredas | Group M |
| 4. | Robert | Winston | Starcom |
| 5. | Linda | Kahn | Ohlmann Group |
| 6. | Kat | Pearson | Graham Oleson |
| 7. | Tom | Meyer | MBMG |

**Seller (Media and/or Representation Firm)**

| | | | |
|---|---|---|---|
| 1. | Jack | Wakshlag | Turner Networks |
| 2. | Trey | Harb | Time Warner Cable Media |
| 3. | Susan | Brami | Spectrum Reach |
| 4. | Marshall | Jacobowitz | Spectrum Reach |
| 5. | Gwen | Throckmorton | Facebook |
| 6. | Nick | Garramone | NCC |
| 7. | Serena | Lal | Yahoo |
| 8. | Art | Salisch | Hearst Argyle Broadcasting |

**Client (Advertiser)**

| | | | |
|---|---|---|---|
| 1. | Blaise | Dsylva | Dr Pepper Snapple |
| 2. | Andrew | Deming | Bank of America |
| 3. | Scott | Hawkins | Lenovo |
| 4. | Denise | Dobyns | Electrolux |
| 5. | Mary Anne | Moldenhauer | Bojangles |
| 6. | Barry | Schrag | Avis/Dominos |
| 7. | Brian | Johnson | Hendrick Automotive |

**Research Vendors (Data/Measurement firm or Advocacy group)**

| | | | |
|---|---|---|---|
| 1. | Sara | Erichson | Nielsen |
| 2. | Jeff | Boehme | RenTrak |
| 3. | George | Ivie | Media Ratings Council |
| 4. | Joe | Matarese | Cadent Technology |
| 5. | Tom | Gombas | Strata/Freewheel |
| 6. | Danielle | Zazula | Comscore |
| 7. | Dennis | Buchheim | Interactive Advertising Bureau |

**Academic (Scholar)**

| | | | |
|---|---|---|---|
| 1. | Esther | Thorson | Michigan State University |
| 2. | Jameson | Hayes | University of Alabama |
| 3. | B.R. | Duff | University of Illinois |
| 4. | Harsh | Taneja | University of Missouri |
| 5. | Jennifer | Romaniuk | University of South Australia |
| 6. | Peter | Danaher | Monash University |
| 7. | Sela | Sar | University of Illinois |
| 8. | Don | Schultz | Northwestern University |

| | |
|---|---|
| **COUNT:** | **37** |

participants did spend large chunks of time in a particular segment (to which they were assigned for purposes of this study), but several of them also moved between segments.

For example, several of the scholars either worked in advertising prior to or during their academic careers, including consulting for industry.  Further, at least one of the professionals had previously worked in academia.  In addition, many professionals worked in different segments throughout the course of their careers.  For example, some of the client/buyers previously worked at advertising agencies or media, and some of the measurement/advocacy participants formerly worked at media or agencies.  There were also examples of agency participants who previously worked as media/sellers.  So, there was a certain amount of fluidity between the segments.  However, at the same time, many of the participants certainly spent the bulk of their time in one particular segment or another.  It's also important to note that, from a qualitative perspective, participant exposure to multiple segments afforded them different views of the advertising "elephant" which added to the richness of their experiences and perspectives about advertising and how it works.

As a reminder, to enhance understanding and explanation, the participants are referred to with a code indicating the segment that each represents.  For example, John Smith from an advertising agency is referenced as John Smith (A).  The coding is as follows:

1.  Buyers/Advertising Agencies (**A**)

2.  Sellers/**Media & Representation Firms (M**)

3.  **Clients/Advertisers (C**)

4.  **Research Vendors/Data, Measurement Firm/Advocacy Group (R**)

5.  Academics/Scholars (**S**)

**Billings/Revenue Representation**

The participants in this study came from a broad spectrum of organizations but, as a whole, they represented a significant volume of advertising in the United States (and several in foreign countries as well).  As advertising is a significant economic driver, it is relevant to understand the level of advertising from a financial perspective that the participants' organizations represented.

The agency participants in this study ranged from individual consultants to those who worked with advertising agencies that had billings of $25-$50 million, $400 to $750 million, and even more than $100 billion annually.

The participants in this study from the media group worked with firms that had annual advertising revenues ranging approximately $500 million to nearly $30 billion.

Meanwhile, participants in the client category worked at companies that had advertising expenditures ranging from $15 million annually to several hundred million dollars per year.

For the measurement/advocacy group participants, advertising billing is not necessarily an indicator of their participation in advertising.  However, their clients and members represented virtually every major (and most minor) advertisers and media players in the United States.  For example, Nielsen represents more than six billion dollars annually in media and measurement services from media, advertisers, and agencies across the world.  Additionally, the Media Rating Council (MRC) counts among its members a significant majority of major advertising organizations, including television networks (e.g., ABC, A&E, Fox, CBS, NBC, ESPN), advertising agencies (e.g., Carat, Magna, Mindshare, Universal McCann, Zenith),  digital entities (e.g., Facebook, Google, Pandora), advertising organizations (4 A's, Advertising Council, Association of National Advertisers), advertising clients (e.g., Bank of America,

Microsoft, Procter & Gamble), and other media companies/organizations (e.g., Apple, Charter Communications, The New York Times, the Radio Advertising Bureau, Time, Inc.).

**Findings by Research Question**

The semi-structured interviews – and subsequent coding – yielded findings that will be presented in the context of each of the four research questions that guided the study.

**Research Question 1: How do advertising professionals view advantages and disadvantages of the impression (CPM) as a single-measure of cross-platform message delivery?**

Susan Brami (M), regional vice president, sales at Spectrum Reach, observed that "at the very basic level, advertising measurement is how many eyeballs are seeing the advertisement." This is a theme that runs throughout the study and was commented on in a similar fashion by multiple participants. Many of the study participants also confirmed that advertising measurement is currently operationalized in many different, siloed, media-specific methods. But they also typically observed that measurement of some sort is critical to the process of buying and selling advertising. Overall – and notably – the participants expressed far more advantages than disadvantages to an impression-based measurement approach.

According to Debbie Basham (A), senior vice president, director of audio and video investment at MediaHub, the advertising industry needs "a currency, a metric to transact against." And one of the primary questions for the advertising community is whether traditional media will continue to be siloed in their measurement or whether the traditional media will move to impression-based measurement (CPM).

**Advantages.** A large majority of the participants agreed that there are benefits to a holistic, cross-platform metric such as the impression.  Benefits include simplicity, comprehensiveness, efficiencies, comparability, and ease of understanding.  For example, Marshall Jacobowitz (M), vice president of audience & product insights at Spectrum Reach, commented that the current system of siloed measurements could be improved if the industry could get to one complete measurement, and "that makes it a lot easier to do effectiveness advertising."  Further, Gwen Throckmorton (M), head of industry at Facebook, observed that a single impression-based metric across advertising platforms "would absolutely be a benefit because you'll be able to actually understand what the triggers are in people's engagement and what actually causes people to convert" because it would help "to truly understand your audience and what ultimately they're responding to about your message."

In addition, as multimedia campaigns are the norm, a single measure of advertising delivery like the impression can help buyers and sellers begin to learn how media act and work (or don't work) together.  According to noted advertising scholar Esther Thorson (S), professor of journalism at Michigan State University,

> When you're looking for the magic and elusive single measurement, it would allow you to then get a truly effective handle on the question, not only of how advertising in one medium works, but how an integrated communication plan works.

Providing insights on the effects of multiple media together are also a benefit of a cross-platform metric observed by Peter Danaher (S), professor of marketing and econometrics at Monash University in Australia.  For Danaher, the ability to gain a deeper understanding of multimedia correlation effects would offer significant value; "That will be the biggest benefit of having this ability to measure all the simultaneous…audiences across multiple different media types."

Harsh Taneja (S), assistant professor of media at the University of Illinois, also commented that impression-based measurement could inject efficiencies into the advertising planning and buying processes.  It would make the whole profession less siloed in terms of platforms and media, like you won't really need a TV planning division, a newspaper planning division -- and digital, which is separate; it would probably help realize a communication plan much better in the form of media plan.  So, mainly, a lot of efficiency gains could be had. Barry Schrag (C), an advertising manager previously with Avis Rent-a-Car and Domino's Pizza, also saw benefits of using the impression as a single advertising delivery metric across media and platforms, "Just knowing in terms of when, and where, and how are the best ways to reach people, to capture attention, to get them to act.  Why wouldn't you want that?"  Art Salisch (M), with Hearst Argyle Broadcasting, added that a single impression-based advertising metric would have great value:

> Because you'd be able to assign media value or monetary value to media on an apples-to-apples comparison – and you could really see deliveries, one against the other, and see which is more effective.  It's one of those things that inevitably makes so much sense on the buying side.

Along those same lines, Mary Anne Moldenhauer (C), senior director of media services at Bojangles' Restaurants, noted that cost comparisons on a CPM basis would be simpler and more reliable because a single metric could deliver "a true cost per thousand… for each medium."

George Mafredas (A), senior partner, director of research at Group M expressed the benefits of a using the impression as a single, cross-platform media metric this way: "It puts everything on an even playing field.  It's as simple as that.  It's video; it's no longer TV, digital. It's video.  It's audio.  It doesn't matter what the delivery system is."  He added that "measurement that can measure across devices and give us the accurate impressions" would be "nirvana." Dennis Buchheim (R), senior vice president & general manager of the Technology Laboratory at the Interactive Advertising Bureau (IAB), continued that theme: "From the marketer's perspective, the benefits would be achieving something much closer to that nirvana we talked about and realizing how to intelligently spend their budgets."

And the benefits would accrue to media, agencies, and clients alike. Good measurement that allows comparison across media can benefit all the players. As Linda Kahn (A), CEO/director, media services at The Ohlmann Group, observed, "We survive together." Scott Hawkins (C), executive director of marketing, Lenovo Data Center Group, echoed that sentiment,

> Everyone in the industry, particularly those who are funding the work and buying the media, would appreciate a common platform that could pull all of that [advertising delivery] in into one view. That would then allow customers like myself to potentially be more involved directly in buying that medium, being able to get that intelligence reported directly back in an aggregated view.

Brami (M) added that multiple media measurement needs a single, specific metric, "I don't see how you sell cross-platform without doing it by impression."

Kat Pearson (A), integrated media manager at the Graham Oleson agency, agreed that impression-based measurement across media would be beneficial, commenting "I don't think it's being done a lot or as much as it should be done. I think that that would be a really easy way to kind of make everything apples to apples." Tom Meyer (A), director of consumer insights at MBMG Media, seemed to represent several participants when he commented "number one, I think impressions are the most basic unit, regardless of media type. But, number two, with my planning hat on I'm not trying to deliver impressions, I'm trying to communicate a message." In essence, he suggested that impressions are necessary but not sufficient. However, both agreed that the impressions (exposure to the message) are a necessary precursor to subsequent measures of effectiveness, including awareness, sales performance, etc. Danielle Zazula (R), vice president of business development at Comscore, concurred. She observed, "you can't get to the, 'What happened next?' if you don't measure advertising [delivery]." As Romaniuk (S) put it, we must ensure "our message gets out to people because we can only ever have an effect on the people that we're reaching."

Impressions are also much more easily understood than more formal media metrics such as gross ratings points (GRPs). Nick Garramone (M), senior vice president eBusiness Operations and Research for NCC Media, argued that the world of advertising is moving to impressions because "an impression is an intuitive measure. You can go to a local car dealer or a local restaurant owner as an example and say, 'Hey. I got an impression.' And they will understand that." Though many across the advertising ecosystem lament the still-siloed nature of advertising measurement, Thorson (S) commented: "people that are interested in measurement are sure looking at it [the impression]." Sara Erichson (R), executive vice president of U.S. Media at Nielsen is one of several ad professionals who believe the shift to impression-based measurement has already begun because of the simplicity of the metric. "There are different definitions across media by how you count it, but an impression is an impression. Impressions are the number of people exposed to the media." Erichson (R) added:

> Essentially, cross-platform data over time will replace television program ratings to drive all the same fundamental business uses that Nielsen ratings data has always played in our clients' offices. And, whether you're a network selling ads or a buyer buying ads, you still want to understand what the whole ecosystem looks like from a planning perspective.

**Disadvantages.**  One specific disadvantage was also suggested regarding the use of the impression as a cross-platform delivery metric.  Jack Wakshlag (M), founder of Media, Strategy, Analytics, and Research, as well as former chief research officer for Turner Broadcasting and head of research for the WB Network, was one who did have a particular concern.  He suggested that three factors (reach, frequency, and duration of message exposure) are "the fundamental measures of advertising."  He referred to these as "How many, how often, how long."  According to Wakshlag, there is one distinct disadvantage to using the impression alone as a cross-platform metric because it doesn't answer all three of those questions.  He stated:

> I don't think impression is enough; it's reach, it's number of impressions, and it's time of exposure.  So, unless you have a broader definition of impression that includes duration, I don't think you'd get to where you need to be, because you can't ignore duration.

Another concern that Wakshlag shared is that impression-based measurement would lack the capability to remove duplicated impressions or to 'de-duplicate' the exposures.  For example, impressions can be summed, but one would not want to count two impressions from the same person (say, via different media) the same way that one counts two impressions from different people – to distinguish reach from frequency.  In standard media math, reach times frequency equals impressions (R x F = IMPs).  Reach (how many) and frequency (how often) are two separate measures that are traditionally calculated for television delivery.  However if one starts with impressions, it's challenging to go backward.  Schrag (C) also thought that "measuring impressions alone probably wouldn't be enough."

Separately, at least two of the participants suggested that more traditional television metrics might more appropriately be applied across media.  For example, Basham (A) shared that buyers sometimes convert advertising schedules into impressions (CPMs), but planners often convert everything to the traditional television measure of ratings (GRPs) – and clients are often

presented cross-platform metrics in the form of GRPs.  Further, Jenni Romaniuk (S), research

professor at the University of South Australia and past editor of the Journal of Advertising

Research, suggested:

> TV's been around a long time, it's going to be around a long time.  It may evolve, but as
>
> a medium it's still in there.  We have basic metrics for TV: reach, frequency, time spent
>
> viewing.  I don't see why they can't be applied to every other medium.

Although not necessarily a disadvantage, these comments did represent an alternative view or

approach other than the impression for cross-platform measurement.

The participants definitely shared broad agreement that the benefits of an impression-

based advertising measurement approach far outweighed potential negatives.  However, the

participants also expressed significant concerns regarding the challenges associated with the

operationalization of an impression-based approach for measuring advertising delivery across

media.  The consensus was that impression-based delivery makes sense and that it should likely

be the way advertising is measured.

**Research Question 2: What are the challenges in creating, implementing, and
adopting an impression-based measurement approach for multiple advertising media?**

The participants suggested several obstacles that might hinder the implementation and

adoption of the impression as a single measure of advertising delivery.  These challenges were

coded to look for patterns to help understand the data (Patton, 2002).  The resultant eight

categories of challenge were: (1) vested interests, (2) standards, (3) comparison, (4) data access,

(5) definition of impression, (6) complexity of media environment, (7) relative valuations, and

(8) cost.

**Vested interests.**  One recurring theme in the area of challenges to moving to an

impression-based advertising measurement approach across media was the existence of legacy

systems and vested interests.  Because advertising is a major economic force, there are immense

financial implications to any change in the existing ecosystem.  But individual players are

sometimes less interested in the overall system than in the impact closer to home.  Duff (S)

observed, "one of the problems is people always have to then see themselves as winners or

losers."  Added Danaher (S), "There would definitely be losers and that's probably why you

haven't seen it [significant movement away from siloed systems]."

With such large amounts of money and extremely high volumes of complex multimedia

advertising, automated systems are an important part of the advertising infrastructure.  If those

systems cannot support the change, then the industry will have a serious challenge moving

toward a common measurement approach.  Tom Gombas (R) vice president, cable division at

Strata/Freewheel clearly stated the problem: "It's the back office that will kill you."  For

example, Basham (A) noted that the Donovan buying system (a popular media buying and

billing software package used by major advertising agencies) does not allow impression-based

buying at the local TV market level.  So, if major agencies (those that process billions of dollars

in advertising) can't implement impression-based buying for television in their systems – which

often represents the most spending – then that is a significant blockage to furthering an

impression-based cross-platform approach.  Simply put: money is a powerful driver.  Salisch (M)

observed, "I think that everybody comes at it from their point of view of how they make their

money and how their business works."  And with an advertising ecosystem spanning the globe, a

host of extant business practices would likely be impacted.  Not surprisingly, players are

reluctant to lose whatever control they think they have.  Erichson (R) observed that media, agencies and other parties might "feel the better business model is to sell separate commercials, separate sales teams, separate pricing, higher CPMs for their premium video and digital platforms."  Changing the existing siloed structure will not be easy.  According to Kahn (A) "You'd really have to have buy-in from every single media partner that you would want to do this with.  And obviously, they all have something else in mind.  They want to sell things the way that it looks best for them, which is one of the reasons why, as an agency, you're very careful to use research that isn't always sponsored by that particular group."  So, is there a path forward to advertising delivery measured by impressions?  Ivie (R) thinks that "the biggest challenge is changing behavior.  Once I have that, I have to sell against the ecosystem that's currently structured, and convince people that my mousetrap will help them."

Even in the digital world, where impressions are the norm, they don't want to change either.  They seem to believe that impressions are the easy answer and that all media should just simply convert.  Taneja (S) asserts "opinions from within the industry are colored by the part of the ecosystem they represent.  I think that Silicon Valley has a very different view on advertising measurement compared to [traditional] media planning and buying agencies.  If I had to use one term to characterize the Silicon Valley, I would say they are anti-television.  So, obviously according to the Silicon Valley, if you stop your allegiance to how advertising was measured and this measurement [impressions] was acted upon in traditional media, they really think that they have it all solved."

But resistance to change is still a major obstacle.  Brami (M) observed that Nielsen, Arbitron, and even digital systems want to continue to do business as they have for years.  "People don't want change. They do not want change," echoed Throckmorton (M).  Clearly, resistance to change is an entrenched blocker of moving toward impression-based buying.

Change is always difficult, especially when there are vested interests involving billions of dollars at stake.  Although virtually every participant expressed dissatisfaction with the current measurement system, they were also somewhat leery of alternatives.  Director of Advertising for Hendrick Automotive Group Brian Johnson's (C) response was typical: "It's just the ambiguity, right?  It's just the unknown."

Multiple vested interests contribute to the lack of progress in moving toward a cross-platform measurement system such as the impression.  Garramone (M) noted, "The challenge right now is there are so many different entities out there with so many agendas."  One of these challenges is the way advertising agencies handle their media activity: still in discrete areas of responsibility.  Salisch (M) commented "Most major agencies, they silo the media as far as buying is concerned.  There are separate people that buy radio than buy TV.  They don't have the same people executing a media plan for multimedia."  Harb (M), director of national sales at Spectrum Reach, added that advertising agency structure itself is "an obstacle to broadening the horizon and looking more cross-platform, even though clients probably would want to."

**Standards.**  Currently, there are different standards for how different media are measured and reported.  "The bar is not the same for everyone. The standard that people may hold for TV, that they may hold for billboards, is much lower than it is for digital," said Throckmorton (M).  Even the amount of time that an advertisement must be seen to count as an impression differs across media.  According to Salisch (M) "online, there is what they call viewability, which is you see something for two seconds and it gets credit.  Now in TV, as you mentioned, local TV, it's five minutes."  The standard for viewing across different media – even for the same video content varies dramatically.  In the example that Salisch mentioned above, the differential is enormous – approaching many thousands of percent.  Hawkins (C) commented on this differential as well, "When Nielsen measures the commercial ratings on their C3 National sample, I think that they've got to be at least 15 seconds, and then some websites are doing like two seconds. And so even... It could be the same 30-second video, but it may or may not be counted at all depending on where it's seen." Indeed, the variability in reporting standards is recognized by others as well. Blaise D'Sylva (C) vice president of media at Dr Pepper Snapple Group further lamented the inconsistency:

> YouTube or Hulu who says, "Hey, we'll measure 30 seconds," and you've got Facebook who says, "We'll measure three," and then you have Snapchat who says, "We're just measuring an impression, so the second it comes up." So you've got all these different pieces and how should they be measured.

The discrepancies in minimum viewing standards across media types are certainly a barrier to a consistent, or 'fair,' cross-platform measurement system.

But there are those who are trying to level the playing field. George Ivie (R) CEO and executive director at Media Rating Council commented "One of the hardest things that we're undertaking with these standards, is setting the processes for deduplicating them. So we're creating reach, in fact, a real reach measure across these devices." (If this could be achieved, then impressions would be able to deliver both reach *and* frequency – accounting for two out of three of Wakshlag's necessary components.)

**Comparison.** Another challenge identified by the several of the participants was how to aggregate and compare impressions from different media. Jacobowitz (M) observed that there is no vetted approach to combine impressions, "no accepted currency cross-media impression methodology." He asked, "How are researchers supposed to compare cross-platform impressions on an even playing field when some of the metrics aren't even in the stadium?"

Meyer (A) observed:

I'd like to believe that there are fundamental building blocks that are identical across

media, and if you look at the root of it, going back to what I said initially, I think you can

talk about individual impressions, and those are pretty consistent across media types. It's

how those impressions are measured; what's the research methodology behind it? Or

how it is aggregated up into reporting. Each media type seems to have a different way of

identifying universes, of identifying segments within those universes to report on.

Harb (M) asked:

How do you compare media to media to media? And how do you compare in a reach and

frequency? How do I know that we reach you on TV, the radio, Pandora, a billboard,

newspaper, direct mail? There's no comparable statistic across all to measure that.

Meyer (A) added:

Because there are numerous independent silos for these media types, it's difficult

to look at the interrelationship of exposure between media. That's not to say that

they don't exist across platform panels, but there is a pretty big problem, because

those panels are nowhere near the scale you need to have absolute confidence in

the breadth of information, because there's so many... There's so much content

and choice now, that it's really hard to have what would be a stable reporting at

that granular a level.

Erichson (R) commented:

Having comparability metrics, I think, is by far the number one priority as you

talk about the differences across platforms. I think that really trumps everything

else. Every medium is measured a little bit differently, and that's okay because each platform is different.  So tailoring the measurement of the platform is okay

to do.  And whether you're Nielsen or someone else, that makes all the sense in

the world to do. But the single biggest thing that companies like Nielsen can

deliver, and what the industry is asking for, is how do you solve for, currently,

different kinds of metrics and across platforms?  How do you make it all talk the

same language?"

The ability to combine, consolidate, and compare impressions from various media and

devices is one of the critical needs to enable impression-based measurement.

**Data access.**  Jacobowitz (M) argued that metrics must be accepted, comparable, and

available.  For example, impression data that Facebook and Google maintain are not made

available to other media or advertisers; and keeping this data privately held inhibits impression-

based advertising.  Throckmorton (M) said:

The biggest obstacle that I can think of is, what is going to be the measuring body, the

Nielsen of the world that actually has, or multiple vendors, that actually provide a

consistent methodology that everybody's willing to sign up for.

Romaniuk (S) added, "lack of transparency makes it really, really hard for someone to be

confident in those systems."  Open access to media viewership data is an accepted part of the

advertising ecosystem for most legacy media.  However, online media doesn't always look at

such data as something that should be shared.  Fielding (A) noted "the Googles and the

Facebooks and the Amazons of the world, which do not view it [data] in that way.  And in fact,

they almost view it in the opposite way."  It's as if they are saying "We don't release our data,

we will not be cooperating with measurement companies because the data we have is of

incredible value to us, and it's proprietary and there's data privacy."  Others also observed accessibility concerns.  For example, according to Boehme (R), accessibility also includes

affordability and time frames of availability.  He stated:

> It's a question of perfecting those systems for consistency and also other, I would say,
>
> pragmatic issues to make sure that the data are affordable, accessible when you want it,
>
> it's speed so that... For example, real time is not available yet.

**Definition of impression.**  Another challenge is that there is disagreement as to exactly

what an impression is.  The simple definition of an impression as a single exposure sounds

straightforward enough, but, according to some, it may be difficult to operationalize.  Schultz

(S), professor (Emeritus-in-Service) of integrated marketing communications at Northwestern

University, argued that we really do not have a functional definition of an impression.  Pearson

(A) claimed that one of the most difficult things "would be getting the different media to agree

upon, 'this is what TV will call an impression, this is what outdoor will call an impression, this is

what digital will call an impression.'" (Such concerns often refer to the aforementioned duration

component.)  Clients also wanted a clearer explanation of what is meant by impression.  D'Sylva

(C) argued that we all need to agree as to what qualifies as an impression.  Brittany Duff (S),

associate professor of advertising at the University of Illinois, went further: "We need a

definition of what 'delivered' is."

**Complexity of media environment.**  The plethora of media options and devices for

audience consumption and advertising use continues to expand and become more complex.

According to Ivie (R), "the biggest one [challenge] is just that consumers are getting much more

complex to measure.  They have many more devices.  The average person has four or five

connected devices on their person and in their household today."

Due to this complexity, many industry players have not been able to keep up.  Further, the measurement infrastructure has not been able to keep pace with the change.  Erichson (R) commented "Our network clients have been concerned for a long time that as they go out there talking about the size of their audience to their programming on TV, that those numbers from Nielsen are missing a portion of their viewing because people are increasingly watching TV on different platforms right now and through different devices."  Danaher (S) agreed that complexity regarding measurement and technology is one of the primary challenges the industry faces.  Schultz (S) also observed that the complexity of today's media environment has outpaced existing tools and techniques.  "Multiple impressions coming from incredible numbers of resources, and people talking to each other, social media and all those kind of things, and so what we've got are old-time models and radically different systems and situations that people are using today," he said.

**Relative valuations.**  If common standards could be developed and if industry players could compare media to each other, there is still the question of economic valuation.  Many participants commented on the challenge of how to assign value to impressions from different media.  Taneja (S) suggested, "the biggest struggle with online measurement has been how to establish equivalence with the ways we were doing this for traditional media."  The worry is that an impression with video and sound is probably worth more than, say, a static impression from a non-moving banner ad.  A similar question might be: 'What is the worth of a radio impression that is sound-only compared to the worth of an impression from a magazine or a newspaper with no sound?'  The participants questioned how relative valuation would be handled.  For example, Schrag (C) doubted the equivalization of comparing cross-platform impressions was possible, saying "in a relative sense, there's no way that you can weight them equally, no way."  Salisch (M) agreed; "Trying to compare a digital impression to a TV impression is, in my mind, it can't be done at this point because of the way the data is." Most agreed with Hawkins (C) who expressed his belief that "some portion of those common-definition impressions would be more valuable than others." Richard Fielding (A), strategic media consultant and former vice president/director of the global research group for Starcom/MediaVest, put it succinctly: "all impressions not are created equal."

Is it the medium itself that creates differentiation? How much does the variability of devices contribute to the differing valuation of impressions? Garramone (M) asks "what is the fundamental qualitative aspect of that specific impression" for a particular media outlet? Advertisers still think that impression-based measurement would be a positive change, but they have the same concerns about valuation across media. Denise Dobyns (C), senior manager of customer relationship marketing at Electrolux, observed "I think using impressions to measure across media is a good idea. You would just have to know that they couldn't be treated equally." Andrew Deming (C), senior communications strategy and brand manager at Bank of America, agreed, and his company has already begun considering advertising using impressions. He explained that his team must now train their internal users, as "We're just converting everything to estimated impression levels, and we're explaining it out that way. The tutorials now change to, 'Not all impressions are created equal.'"

Gombas (R) suggested that the potential commoditization of ad delivery based on impressions could represent a serious financial risk if the relative valuation is not included in the mix. He asserted, "Just blindly turning into a CPM business, or an impression-selling business, without really staying focused on the value and differentiation between the media types, could lead to just racing to the bottom of the CPM pricing schedule." In other words, media risk commoditization – which limits revenue potential.

An extended piece of the relative valuation discussion is context.  It's important for marketers to understand message delivery in the context of the universe in which those messages are delivered.  Garramone (M) commented:

> Impressions by themselves don't really make that much sense without context.  Because if you've got 100,000 impressions but there were 4 million people in the marketplace, you really didn't get that much exposure.  But if you've got, let's say, 1 million impressions and there are 2 million people, you can have an intuitive sense of delivery.  Those million impressions were seen by 40% of the market on average 2 1/2 times.  Then you get to reach and frequency which are other important components of media measurement.

**Cost.**  There is a cost to any form of data measurement – and one challenge acknowledged by various study participants is that sometimes the cost could be prohibitive.  According to Robert Winston (A) "from a very practical standpoint, measurement is expensive…  It's very, very expensive."  Impression-based measurement is not used for many media currently, so it would have to be created.  Who will bear this additional cost?  Not only would the creation of the measurement infrastructure be needed, but resources would need to be allocated for players to use the data.  This would be an additional cost in an era when advertising agencies have reduced spending.  As Thorson (S) observed, "It used to be that ad agencies all had a research department, now none of them have a research department."  While this may be an exaggeration, her point is that resource cutbacks in the agency community have been significant; this emphasizes the relevance of the cost challenge.

In summary, the participants offered eight challenges for creating, implementing, and adopting an impression-based measurement approach on a cross-platform basis.  The eight categories included vested interests, standards, comparison, data access, definitions, complexity of media environment, relative valuations, and cost.

**Research Question 3: What additional considerations will need to be addressed regarding media measurement in light of the dynamic media environment?**

When prompted, participants shared additional ideas that would need to be part of the path forward for measurement in an ever-changing media landscape. These supplemental considerations were generally more downstream and more environmental in nature than the initial obstacles suggested in response to RQ2; further, these concerns also often went beyond the actual measurement of advertising. The seven over-arching additional considerations for media measurement suggested by the study participants included (1) the enormity of the task at hand (Scale), (2) the rise of data science and its integration into the marketing world (Data Science vs. Media & Marketing), (3) the changes in media and the media ecosystem (Media Evolution), (4) the problem of data kept behind firewalls away from other media and advertisers (Walled Garden), (5) making better, more relevant content for advertising messages (Creative), (6) non-human traffic or false reporting of advertising delivery (Fraud), and (7) distraction due to new developments (Bright, Shiny, New Things).

**Scale.** Buchheim (R) observed that the desire to measure cross-platform has to take into account the volume of data and the differences across media and platforms;

> Let's take for granted you want to measure it, you're motivated to measure it; how do you do it when the interaction models are very different? Whether talking about ads and apps, which can be a little bit different, or video ads versus audio ads, versus something you see on the TV, versus just on your tablet or a phone versus the desktop, versus a laptop. It's all different. And I think that has become almost paralyzing.

The reaction of 'analysis paralysis' is certainly a risk as media, platforms, and data continue to proliferate. Johnson (C) commented "I don't know if the metric is the challenge. It's the data…it's unlocking the data and harnessing the data that's the challenge." The huge scale of the data (aka 'big data'), as well as the variability of data types and measurement methods, can be bewildering to even seasoned researchers and data scientists.

Volume is also a concern at the consumer level. According to Jacobowitz (M), "The other area that's becoming a concern, it seems like it's less of a public concern now, even though it should probably be more of a public concern than it has been, at least, in my opinion, is clutter." Clutter is a word to describe too many messages hitting somebody over a period of time. He went on to say:

> I remember when I was first in the industry, and we would see press releases, or we would get mailings from organizations that said, 'The average person is seeing 28 to 30 messages a day,' and they thought that was too much. Whereas, we know now, people are probably getting 200 to 300 messages a day, between the Internet, and between television, and all their mobile devices, and all the place-based media, which really didn't exist 20 years ago.

Throckmorton (M) observed that media proliferation is affecting media consumption; "at the end of the day the only thing that's scarce is time, and people are fitting more consumption, especially certain people, into that same 24 hours of the day." Not only are media proliferating – it seems there's a new 'app' around every corner – users adopt and discard media at a much faster pace. Kahn (A) noted:

> Things are way different than they were 40 years ago, and they're constantly changing at a much greater pace, and I don't think that we're indicative of being different than the

world is.  It's a constant evolution, a constant change.  Facebook is not your child's

Facebook any longer, that's a perfect example.  The minute we all got turned onto it, our

kids said, "No thanks, I've moved on; I'm on something else now."

All of this volume – of data and of consumer usage and new media that continue to

evolve – represent a significant measurement challenge that the industry has not yet resolved.

Sela Sar (S) associate professor of advertising at the University of Illinois speculated "I think

that it will be very difficult to answer whether or not we can really be able to catch up with that

measurement."

**Data science vs. media & marketing.**  Several participants suggested that dealing with

'big data' – the specialty of data science – brings both benefits and challenges into the media

measurement sphere.  On the one hand you have the marketers, the traditional media people, and

then, on the other hand, you have the data scientists.  They tend to have different perspectives on

the world.  The data scientists (who are generally more likely to be from the digital realm) think

that as long as you can get enough data, you can get a good answer.  Meanwhile, the marketers

tend to be a little more skeptical. They ask questions of why, and what specifically are you

measuring, and can you really just say A plus B equals C?

For example, Jeff Boehme (R), chief client officer at Rentrak commented that "the rise of

the data scientist is important and necessary but data scientists are not by definition researchers,

and the problem is interpreting the data.  So that you can have good data scientists, understand

everything about the data set but have no idea about the practical application of it."  Further,

Schultz (S) suggested that "the data scientists have brought a lot of power, a lot of number

crunching ability to understand big data, to the forefront.  But they often tend to lack some of the

subtleties of media."  The participants saw opportunities for the data scientists and the media and marketing researchers to work together.  At the same time, they also saw competition between these two groups.

Wakshlag (M) commented:

The challenge of bringing together two groups of people that have different traditions, the people from digital analytics versus people from media research is that their backgrounds are different.  The guys who do digital analytics are generally really strong in mathematics and modeling.  They can take data in any way, shape or form, start processing it, and come up with a decent way of looking at it, to know and understand what has happened.  Also, if they're smart, they take that data and try to project it forward so they can start estimating with it, and predicting the future with it.  And they're quite good at that.  But what they don't have is an understanding of the quality of the data.  It could be good data, it could be bad data.  They treat it largely the same, while someone in media research is usually highly concerned with the quality of the data, as well as the analytics.  So the media researcher is generally less sophisticated in mathematics and modeling, a less good data manipulator than somebody who's in digital analytics, but have a better and deeper understanding and knowledge of the quality of the data they're working with, and its limits.

Some participants agreed with Jacobowitz (M), who suggested media has:

Done really well, I think, at measuring exposure.  Yes, it's mainly siloed, and we haven't done the cross-platform, but there are a lot of people working on that cross-platform.  And because we have all the data – we have a lot of data – more than we've ever had, it feels like it's solvable.  Throw enough processing power at it, and somebody will figure it

out.

Other participants agreed with Boehme (R) on the risks of blindly following data when he

commented that "the data scientist role is, I think, really, really smart, but dangerous if not

managed correctly."  According to Romaniuk (S), the fallacy is that if you have enough data that

you can solve any problem – "Right, which is not the case.  Big, biased data is not better than

small unbiased data."

Joe Matarese (R), chief technologist at Cadent Technology, wondered "how you fill in

those gaps between I think what the marketing people can sense could happen based on their

experiences and what the data scientists just know how to turn the cranks in terms of output."

One way to begin to address the disconnect between data scientists and media/marketing

professionals was suggested by Hayes (S), assistant professor of advertising and public relations

at the University of Alabama.  He declared:

> What needs to happen from the academic point of view is, there need to be programs
>
> developed that will train communication people in data science, because the problem is,
>
> those data scientists can look at the numbers, but they have zero clue how to tell a story
>
> with those numbers for the brand.  They don't understand communication enough to do
>
> that.  They can tell you statistics, but they can't translate the data into a story.

**Media evolution.**  To a large degree, media and platforms are changing at such a rapid

pace that it is difficult for anyone to keep up.  In this 'app every other day' environment of new

and emerging media, platforms, and devices, measurement is often thought of well after the

latest technology is launched – when there is a subsequent attempt to monetize the new app, or new media, or the device.  As media evolve, there are a host of new challenges for those who are

interested in measurement.  Meyer (A) observed:

> Part of it is there are apps and tools that are in the ad-blocker space that are really
>
> popular.  So, number one, people are blocking ads because there's something that bugs
>
> them about the ads.  So, for starters, you kind of need to make ads that people would
>
> actually welcome.

Some commented on the difference between traditional media and new forms of media like

'search' (e.g., Google, Yahoo, Bing, and other Internet paid search utilities) that are user-driven.

Brami (M) observed:

> Historically, media for the most part has been other information, entertainment
>
> that people consume.  And ads are integrated somehow; you're looking at
>
> something else, to get you to look at the ad.  Now billboards, interestingly, are
>
> different because they're the ad.  But often they're informational, this exit here or
>
> whatever.  Now, we're moving to search –and there's no other information really;
>
> it's just what you want, and there may be ads on the side or whatever, but then
>
> you get into some of this stuff, it's definitely nothing but ads.  So, how do you see
>
> that affecting media?  Is media going to evolve?  Should media and advertising
>
> include the same stuff?  Are we even talking about the same thing?  Is it different
>
> things or is it still an ad being a message from a seller of some sort to a buyer of
>
> some sort?

Garramone (M) thought that patterns of media and platform usage will emerge sooner

rather than later and that the media themselves will be active participants in the measurement

evolution.  He suggested:

Eventually, meaning that over the next three years, it's going to become fairly clear as to where things are heading from a consumption perspective. The end user, what is he or she going to be consuming? Both professional video that we deliver as the MVPDs [multichannel video programming distributor], or through other means like even over the top like Netflix and Amazon, and then other like social, etcetera. It's going to become pretty clear over the next three years where things are heading, not to say that it's going to be perfectly clear. I believe that from a measurement standpoint, entities are going to take the leadership role. It's going to be mostly sell-side entities who are going to step in and say, 'This is how we suggest measuring all of our media.'

Some study participants suggested that the changes in media are going to happen even more quickly, and that many in the industry are unprepared. Schultz (S) commented:

You're going to be talking to a lot of people who believe it's going to change maybe gradually and that, "I'll have time to adapt. I'll have time to adjust," and historically, they have, but I'm not sure they're going to have that in the future.

Most agreed with Gombas (R) when he said "the reality is it's the consumer consumption changes that are going to really drive this. I actually think there are going to be even platforms that will become media platforms that we don't even contemplate today."

Dobyns (C) said:

We just need more people to make decisions based on the data and be willing to test and see what happens when they test based on data decisions instead of "this is how we've always done it" or "this is what I'm most comfortable with" or "this is what I know about."

According to some interviewees, one of the key trends in video, for example, will be how consumers access it.  Boehme (R) clearly believed in the power of video: "Fundamentally, video is critical, so fundamentally following the consumer video consumption patterns are the key." Some of the participants were already watching how these consumer patterns are playing out and how they are changing.  D'Sylva (C) noted, "people actually aren't streaming as much on desktop anymore and they're doing it through their big screens.  Yeah, they're doing it through their big screens.  So I think it's all gravitating back to that."  Others shared trends of technology and consolidation.  For example, Deming (C) commented:

> I think everything will continue to be more digitized.  I think everything's going to migrate more toward one-to-one delivery.  And I think the biggest change that's going to take place is how many players, frankly, are in the industry, and that's going to impact how fast the change takes shape.  And by players, I mean, who else is Facebook going to acquire?  Who else is Google going to acquire? You're already starting to see the inroads of a handful of major players.

Fielding (A) sees the major digital players as very different from traditional media.  He explained:

> One of the issues is you've got what I would say is the emergence of these new platforms that are ecosystems, but they also are media... They are media, but they're a lot of other things as well.  I would include companies like Facebook and Google and Amazon... I'm just trying to think about the way to categorize them…They're the platform.  Exactly.  Yes, they are.  And you notice that these are becoming very dominant players.  I still believe that at the end of the day, it will boil down to Apple, Facebook, Google, and Amazon.  They're everything.

They're the media, they're the delivery, they're the content – and the measurement.

Such consolidation of all aspects of media, content, delivery, and measurement present challenges to an industry that relies on data and openness.  It seems clear that media will continue to evolve.  It's also likely that new measurement schemes will be proposed.  Further, questions of data accessibility are not going away.  Adopting a simple, comparable, cross-platform metric such as the impression might help the advertising industry manage the evolution.

**Walled garden.**  Another theme that emerged from the interviews was the idea that the current media environment is characterized by some parties that are unwilling to share data.  This evolution of some, especially digital, media entities into self-contained systems that do not share data has impacts across the advertising and measurement ecosystem.  Wakshlag (M) observed:

> In the television world, everybody uses a third party, and it's a syndicated data system.  So NBC knows exactly how many people watch CBS, or at least they have an estimate, a reasonably good estimate.  And that estimate is largely used to relate to the currency, and the advertising, and ad impressions, etcetera, etcetera.  There is a pretty good correlation between audience size and ad impressions, program audience.  But now you can get individual apps.  The problem on the digital side is nobody knows what anyone else is doing.

Lack of information affects audience estimates, share of voice, and other metrics.  But a few powerful players are impacting media and measurement in a way that's different than has historically been the case.  For example, as Fielding (A) observed, "Apple is a huge walled garden because that's their fundamental business philosophy.  They will not and they do not share data, and they won't."

But at least one participant thought there might be negative consequences of this lack of openness back onto the digital entities that take this approach.  Garramone (M) suggested:

Digital only is going to struggle.  They will continue to grow from a revenue standpoint. But I think they're going to struggle on the measurement side because I don't believe they've got a strong voice out there to be able to create harmony outside of Google and Facebook.  I think that the pure play digital players are going to struggle around that measurement piece.  And Google and Facebook are going to continue to say, "We're Google and Facebook and do what we tell you and have a nice day."

**Creative.**  Many study participants suggested that the content of commercials needs to evolve to be more relevant to consumers.  Throckmorton's (M) comments were typical:

What has to change is I think a lot of advertisers have to get really intentional and rigorous about having learning agendas and testing plans that aren't going to have a silver bullet mentality.  Even the Super Bowl isn't the Super Bowl anymore. And you have to understand what consumers are looking for, what state of mind they're in, in each platform – and film creative and learning that ties all those people together.  But when you understand what those triggers are and you can build a plan then you're going to have to just really stay true on what that messaging is and who that audience is in each of those environments.

However, Throckmorton added that specific messaging may be fleeting: "I think creative gets much more perishable now and I think strategies can become quickly inefficient."  Serena Lal (M) director of demand strategy at Yahoo suggested:

We need to actually start building better ad units.  I think it's up to publishers, as soon as we start measuring everything the right way, then I think it becomes up to publishers to create content and ads that their consumers want to see.

In short, the content is relevant. Customized content is more relevant to specific target audiences. D'Sylva (C) said, "I'll tell you something that I always gravitate back to when I talk to people which, coming from a media guy, might seem almost blasphemous, which is, as a brand marketer, it still just comes down to the idea." Ivie (R) agreed, "We need to deliver content and advertising that's more relevant to the consumer in a targeted way, if we want to keep consumers interested."

**Fraud.** Another of the concepts that surfaced with almost every study participant from across the advertising ecosystem was the topic of fraud. Fraud is impressions that aren't real – or aren't from real people. They could be so-called bot traffic or bad data or outright misleading reporting. But whatever the reasons, advertisers do not want to pay for impressions that weren't delivered. One advertising client participant [name withheld upon request for this comment] referred to the digital advertising ecosystem as "nebulous" and a "cesspool of fraud."

Dobyns (C) commented, "We talked a little bit about fraud and the distrust of the data that's out there. I think that we need to get a lot more transparency in how that information is captured." Concerns abound from all of the industry segments. For example, Basham (A) asserted that the industry needs "to be able to do a whole lot better job of measuring the fraud and knowing what it is." Buchheim (R) noted the insidious impact of fraud was that "you can't have accurate measurement if a good chunk – or really any significant portion – of the ads you're delivering are fraudulent." Lal (M) wants to fix the problem:

I would require the ability to filter out the fraud. I think that's a really big deal in digital. Probably less with other marketing channels. But I think that the fraud, non-human traffic, to certain publisher websites is probably always going to be there. And something that I think any cross-platform measure should be able to just eliminate or minimize.

Most of the industry professionals in the study were well aware of inaccurate reporting and even

incorporated it into their planning and buying.  For example, Hawkins (C) shared:

> With the stories that you find in the industry where there has been fraud around those
>
> measurements, it's kind of a given in the industry that you have to assume some of that
>
> risk when you're investing in digital advertising.

> Still, others spoke about the real impacts that fraud has on the measurement system.  For

example, Wakshlag (M) talked about "the technical challenges of making sure the data comes

through and comes through clean, and is of high quality.  That an impression is actually an

impression and not fraud."  Ivie (R) also commented on the "difficulty, just the complexity of

measurement itself, things like invalid traffic and fraud in digital."  Fraud – or lack of reliability

– is a real and growing issue among advertisers and the advertising community.

**Bright, shiny, new things.**  There is also a danger that new technology can be

distracting, according to some study participants.  The flavor of the moment can get in the way

of real measurement and successful advertising and advertising measurement.  Throckmorton

(M) expressed the concern this way: "I just think it's going to be really easy to get fascinated

with the bright, shiny toy, with a bright, shiny thing."  Along those lines, Wakshlag (M) offered

that advertising professionals need to be careful to try to "avoid, what I call, the bright shiny

objects, because we're fascinated by bright shiny objects."  In addition, Zazula (M) observed that

the new tools/opportunities/media keep coming.  "You name it," she said, "there's so much ad

technology out there that we get so caught up with shiny new objects to the left."  And one could

add those shiny objects on the right, those in the middle, etc.  Much of media is at the forefront

of the digital evolution/revolution and technology plays a major role in new forms of media and delivery devices.  As such, bright, shiny distractions are likely to continue.

In conclusion, there were seven additional topics the study participants identified that need to be addressed in today's dynamic media environment.  The seven were scale; data science vs. media & marketing; media evolution; walled garden; creative; fraud; and bright, shiny, new things.

**Research Question 4: What are commonalities and differences among practitioners and academics regarding the topic of a single media delivery measurement and its implementation?**

As indicated earlier, one goal of this study was to include and investigate practitioner perspectives in addition to academic perspectives regarding challenges with effective measurement of advertising delivery and, more specifically, the potential of an advertising impression-based measurement approach (AIM).  Commonalities and/or differences between the two groups with regard to advertising impression measurement were addressed in response to RQ4.

Five primary areas were recognized in which the commonalities and differences between practitioners (who conduct advertising activities) versus academics (who study the topic) showed significant relevance: (1) why advertising is measured, (2) using impressions as a cross-platform metric, (3) challenges for impression-based measurement, (4) current concerns with advertising measurement, and (5) the evolution of advertising and measurement.  The current study found both similarities and differences in these five main areas.  Often, scholars and practitioners are perceived to have differing perspectives on advertising, how it works, and what the field needs.  This is generally thought to be the case because the two groups have different goals and look at advertising through different lenses.  According to one scholar, practitioners are ultimately tied to whatever can be implemented reliably at scale. Meanwhile, those in the academic community are free to look at the data, variables, and scenarios; ask questions; and then theorize as to possible explanations and relationships. The findings from RQ4 illustrate these differences and similarities.

**Scholars: Why advertising is measured.** Collectively, scholars answered the question of why advertising should be measured in terms of three primary reasons: (1) assessment of activities, (2) output, and (3) to see if it works.

*Assessment of activities.* Duff (S) was one scholar who suggested that advertising needs to be assessed:

> We need to understand who we're reaching, if we're reaching people, why we're reaching them, how, when, where. I think one of the problems, of course, is there's no real agreement still on what an appropriate outcome is for communications. So there is kind of a broad talk of, "Oh, of course, it should be communication objectives." It should be things that we can actually achieve with communication.

Responses in this vein were primarily concerned with measuring activities associated with advertising, but the rationale for doing so was not specifically called out.

*Output.* Meanwhile, others suggested the reason for measuring advertising is to understand the output and use it to compare against competitors. For example, Taneja (S) commented "We spend a lot on it [advertising], so why is measuring output important? I think because, if you don't have standardized measures of output, you would never know how you are doing versus your competitors who are advertising." Measures of output most often include simple counts of productivity, including number of commercials, volume of digital, radio, etc. advertisements. Output measures could also include elements such as pre-testing and audience or survey reporting as well as ROI calculations based on sales/revenue. One question for consideration is what are the appropriate output measures for advertising?

*Does it work?* Finally, the third primary reason scholars offered for measuring advertising was to judge effectiveness. Thorson's (S) response is representative "You want to know if it works, that's the bottom line. So, you don't want to spend a bunch of money on an advertising campaign and have that money be wasted. You have to measure responses to advertising – and they need to be as closely related to your advertising strategy as possible." As discussed above, effectiveness is highly variable and largely dependent upon the original advertising goals (and if they were explicitly stated). Further, effectiveness has been shown to be notoriously difficult to just and to quantify.

**Practitioners: Why advertising is measured.** On the other hand, practitioners had largely differing explanations for measuring advertising; most of them agreed that it was important to measure advertising based on the financial investment. They suggested four major reasons to measure advertising: (1) return on investment (ROI), (2) wise spending, (3) optimization, and (4) transactional value. It's important to note that these reasons are often closely related and the rationale for each sometimes crosses into and is linked to the others.

*Return on investment.* The most common rationale suggested by practitioners for measuring advertising was a return on the financial expense of the advertising investment. Erichson (R) was succinct: "The bottom line is, anyone who's going to spend money advertising, no matter what platform, needs to understand what the return is on their investment." Similarly, Jacobowitz (M) commented on the motivation to measure advertising: "It's important to measure because people spend a lot of money on it. And whenever people spend money on something, they want to make sure they get value for their money." Lal (M) agreed, "it's important because you want to know that the budget you deployed actually generated some kind of a return."

Others were more descriptive.  Wakshlag (M) said:

> If you can't measure it, you really don't know the value you're getting.  So it's important
> that you understand and know how advertising expenditures are contributing to your
> company's profitability.  Advertising expenditure is your investment, and the assumption
> is that for every dollar spent on advertising, there's a return in profit of more than a
> dollar.

According to Fielding (A), in business, advertising is one part of the marketing mix and must be evaluated just like any other investment.  He said:

> It's a hugely important part of the marketing process of which brands, products,
> and services are trying to communicate their features and benefits, and are trying
> to influence consumer behavior for consumers to purchase their products and
> services.  So if you take advertising as a hugely important component of the
> marketing process, significant resources and investment are put behind it.  Like
> anything else, you can't manage what you can't measure. Therefore, the
> measurement of the activity and then the response of the activity are essential.
> And so in a way, you can get a measurement of the return on that investment.

In the end, Kahn (A) wrapped up the practitioner viewpoint: "So everybody's asking, 'Gee, if I spend this dollar, how is it going to trickle down?  How is it going to come back to me?'" ROI is a critical metric for the practitioner community.

*Wise spending.*  Practitioners want – and are often required – to prove that they are spending money intelligently.  Buchheim (R) summarized the responses of many practitioners as to why measurement of advertising is important.  He observed, "a drive to understand, as an advertiser or marketer, whether your money is being spent intelligently; are you spending it in the right places?" Meyer (A) outlined the process from the agency perspective: "our clients trust us to take their media budgets and use them wisely. And we plan media, present what we believe are the best uses of their money, and the deliveries are the proof." There is an inherent need (and sometimes audit requirement) to document and justify expenditures in the practitioner world. This is true for every department of advertising and doubly true for every advertising agency.

*Optimization.* When marketers use advertising, they want to do it well. The participants expressed a desire to improve, to get better. Schrag (C) put it this way: "Well, it's important to measure anything you do in life. If you don't measure, you have no yardstick, in terms of what you did was successful or not, also to learn, in terms of how to optimize for moving forward." Dobyns (C) suggested:

> A marketing department is tasked with certain goals like meeting certain sales goals or certain brand health goals. And the only way to know if you're getting close to meeting those goals is if you are able to measure and track your efforts all along. Plus, the reality of marketing is it's expensive to buy advertising. And whatever you're buying, you want to make sure you're using those funds wisely. So you have to be able to measure in order to know what the best tactics are for what you're trying to achieve.

Gombas (R) summarized how everyone involved in the advertising ecosystem is trying to improve performance:

> The old story was half your advertising works; you just don't know which half. I think that at some level we are all still trying to just answer that question. Marketers, agencies,

and clients are all trying to find more efficient ways to communicate, advertise.
Advertisers are under constant and growing pressure to get the most value for their advertising
expenditures. Being able to achieve optimal – or at least improved – results (delivery, attitude
change, etc.) for the same amount of money is a common goal.

*Transactional value.* Finally, several participants also expressed the importance of
measurement to establish value for transactions – the buying and selling of advertising. Basham
(A) offered, "We have to have a currency, a metric to transact against. Without measurement,
you don't have that." Moldenhauer (C) agreed that buyers and sellers need a representation of
value for the purchasing of advertising. "If you don't have a currency there's nothing to
negotiate with."

Salisch (M) concurred that measurement helps to create and maintain the economic cycle
with advertising:

> The main thing is really proving that there's some monetary value. It starts a negotiation
> right there where without research you wouldn't have a clue, the buyer and/or the seller,
> wouldn't have a clue what the 'value' of the advertising space would be – and the
> research leads to being able to create the market place.

Scholars and practitioners agreed that measuring advertising was important, but their
rationale for the measurement was different. Scholars focused on assessment of activities,
output, and effectiveness. Meanwhile, practitioner reasons for measuring advertising were ROI,
wise spending, optimization, and transactional value.

**Using Impressions as a Cross-Platform Metric.** In general, both scholars who study
advertising and professionals who practice advertising thought that there were mostly advantages
to using impressions as a cross-platform metric. (Note that this section of Research Question 4 is

actually a segmentation of the opinions expressed in Research Question 1, but here they are dissected between practitioners versus scholars.)

*Advantages*.  Practitioners, including Garramone (M), Jacobowitz (M), and Throckmorton (M), noted that the simplicity of impressions and the capability of applying impressions across all media vehicles and platforms was a major advantage.

Practitioners (Salisch (M), Buchheim (R), Mafredas (A), Hawkins (C), and Moldenhauer (C)) as well as scholars (Thorson (S) and Danaher (S)) all commented that impression-based cross-platform measurement would allow for true comparisons across media enabling optimization opportunities of integrated advertising campaigns.

Practitioner Zazula (R) and scholar Romaniuk argued that message delivery (impression) is a necessary precursor to any other measurement.  This has been observed and stated multiple times throughout the study, but it cannot be over-emphasized.  The false assumptions of delivery have led the research community to an over-abundance of psychologically-based theories and studies of advertising.

Both practitioner Erichson (R) and scholar Thorson (S) observed that the shift to impression-based measurement has already begun.  Some agencies and buying services, as well as some media, have begun to articulate a need for impression-based measurement, but vested interests continue to challenge progress toward that end.

Separately, Taneja (S) also observed that impression-based measurement could inject efficiencies into the overall advertising planning and buying processes.

So there is broad agreement from both scholars and practitioners as to the benefits of an impression-based measurement approach for advertising.

*Disadvantages*.  Wakshlag (R) and Romaniuk (S) argued that impressions would be insufficient for measurement because they do not encompass all three necessary requirements for advertising delivery: how many, how often, and how long.  Basham (A) and Romaniuk (S) both suggested that existing television metrics might be an alternative suitable cross-platform metric. While this was a minority view, it was shared by a small number of practitioners and academic participants alike.

Though there were few recorded disadvantages to using impressions as a cross-platform media metric, similar concerns were expressed by both the scholars and the practitioners.

**Challenges for impression-based measurement.**  Collectively, scholars and practitioners identified eight categories of challenges to creating/implementing impression-based measurement: (1) vested interests, (2) standards, (3) comparison, (4) data access, (5) definition of impression, (6) complexity of media environment, (7) relative valuations, and (8) cost.  (Note that this section of Research Question 4 is a segmentation of the opinions expressed in Research Question 2, but here they are dissected between practitioners versus scholars.)

Both practitioners and scholars tended to agree on six out of eight of the challenges to impression-based measurement.  Only two challenges to impression measurement (standards and comparability) were challenges recognized by practitioners alone.

Thorson (S) observed that advertising professionals "tend to not like to generalize.  So everything you give that's a measurement or proposed measurement or something like that, they can always think about a huge number of exceptions where that wouldn't work."

Duff (S), Danaher (S), Taneja (S), Gombas (R), Salisch (M), Harb (M), Basham (A), Erichson (R), Ivie (R), and other participants all argued that vested interests in the media ecosystem represent a significant obstacle to the adoption and implementation of an impression-based measurement system.

Only practitioners – Throckmorton (M), Salisch (M), Hawkins (C), D'Sylva (C), and Ivie (R) – identified lack of standards as an obstacle to moving forward with an impression-based measurement approach.

Again, only practitioners – Jacobowitz (M), Meyer (A), Harb (M), Erichson (R) – observed lack of comparison ability (to normalize impressions across media types) as a challenge for impression-based measurement.

Boehme (R), Fielding (A), Throckmorton (M), and Romaniuk (S) noted that lack of open access to data is a hindrance to moving toward an impression-based measurement system.

Both scholars and practitioners – Schultz (S), Pearson (A), D'Sylva (C), and Duff (S) – cite the lack of a commonly accepted definition of the term impression as an impediment to adopting impression measurement across media types.

Again, scholars and practitioners – Ivie (R), Erichson (R), and Schultz (S) – allege that the complexity of the media environment is a hurdle that impression-based measurement must overcome.

At least one scholar (Taneja (S)), joined numerous practitioners (Schrag (C), Salisch (M), Hawkins (C), Garramone (M), Fielding (A), Dobyns (C), Deming (C), and Gombas (R)) in the opinion that how to assign relative valuations to different types of media would be a significant challenge.

Both Winston (A) and Thorson (S) commented that cost of an impression-based cross-platform measurement system might prove problematic for users.  As with any new approach, there are real costs that must be borne by users of the data.  The question of who will absorb these potential new expenses and how the cost will be shared have yet to be answered.

Both scholars and practitioners largely agreed on many of the impediments to an impression-based measurement approach – with both groups identifying 75% of the same challenge areas.

**Current Concerns.**  Participants identified as many as a dozen concerns with advertising measurement in today's media environment.  However, four over-arching categories of concerns rose to the top for practitioners: cross-platform differences, lack of standards, data volume (and how data is handled), and trust.  Meanwhile, the concerns suggested by scholars aligned somewhat with their three most common challenges.  Similar to practitioners, academics identified cross-platform differences as a major concern, but the biggest challenge from the academic perspective was the potential disconnect between measurement systems and the goal of the measurement.  Separately, several of the scholarly participants identified a current concern as a question of what is measured with advertising versus what ought to be measured with advertising.

*Cross-platform differences.*  Differences across media, as well as the continuing evolution of media and devices, create challenges for measurement.  Most media organizations and their leaders want to measure themselves based on their own specific attributes; however, most practitioners long for a view of media across platforms.

Garramone (M) observed:

I think the biggest challenge right now is that media are expanding so rapidly and the complexity of the ability for an individual to consume media whether it's print or video or social or whatever it is, is expanding so fast that measurement is really struggling right now.

According to Fielding (A), a major problem with the "never-ending fragmentation of media delivery and consumption is that, from a measurement perspective, it always seems like the measurement companies are playing catch-up."

Ivie (R) agreed when he said:

One of the biggest challenges is tracking what consumers do and how they consume media is becoming increasingly difficult from a tech and diversity perspective. So just the way people consume media is becoming more and more fragmented. The devices they use, the multitasking they engage in, the way they consume media, much more individually today rather than as a group like, let's say, in front of a TV set after dinner. They still do that, but less so than they used to. So there's one silo of difficulty, which has to do with consumer behavior and the way consumers consume media.

Buchheim (R) commented on the challenge of accounting for cross-platform differences in a multi-media measurement approach:

Let's take for granted you want to measure it, you're motivated to measure it, how do you do it when the interaction models are very different? Whether talking about ads and apps, which can be a little bit different, or videos ads versus audio ads, versus something you see on the TV, versus just on your tablet or a phone versus the desktop, versus a laptop. It's all different. And I think that has become almost paralyzing.

Many of the practitioners' opinions aligned with Wakshlag (M), who asked, "How do you compare media to media to media? And how do you compare reach and frequency? How do I know that we reach you on TV, the radio, Pandora, a billboard, newspaper, direct mail?

There are no comparable statistics across all media to measure that." Practitioners want to be able to compare media directly to each other.

Further, Jacobowitz (M) observed that existing siloed measurement had not been stitched together in any meaningful way. He suggested:

> The industry has done a good job of measuring in a silo for a particular media. So we have good TV measurement, we have good print measurement, we have pretty good radio measurement, we've got pretty good online measurement, but we don't have pretty good measurement of how all those things work together and deliver a single message, or influence a certain respondent or a certain member of the population or the target audience together, and what the unified message in effect is of that brand's advertising. So that's one area where I think people are trying to get to: cross-platform.

Erichson (R) summed up the practitioner perspective, "the number one thing is comparability of the measurement across platforms. I think that really trumps everything else."

Some scholars also observed cross-platform differences as a challenge. From the academic viewpoint, Sar (S) asked how the industry can transition old measurement approaches into the current world and whether "impression measurements can be used cross-platform." Danaher (S) also commented on "the multimedia angle" with all its complexities as a challenge for cross-platform measurement.

***Lack of standards.*** Multiple practitioners called out lack of standards across media as an important challenge with today's advertising environment. Garramone (M) observed "the lack of uniformity across all of the measurement types." Johnson (C) expressed frustration that was typical of the client perspective, "it's all over the place. There are not really consistent standards." Boehme (R) also called for clarification in the areas of "definition of the standards that are different." Meyer's (A) response was even more in-depth:

> I'd like to believe that there are fundamental building blocks that are identical across media, and if you look at the root of it, I think you can talk about individual impressions, and those are pretty consistent across media types. It's how those impressions are measured, what's the research methodology behind it? Or how is it aggregated up into reporting? So, each media type seems to have a different way of identifying universes, of identifying segments within those universes to report on.

Of course, this lack of standards seems to create frustration across the ecosystem, especially for advertisers and agencies that want to utilize and compare multiple media. Interestingly, standards (which would be necessary for implementation) were not suggested as a concern by the scholar participants.

*Data volume*. Concerns about the enormous volume of data were expressed across most of the practitioner subgroups. These concerns fell into two areas: dealing with huge amounts of data and the competing perspectives that drive data analytics. While clients were more concerned about data volume, those in the media and research communities expressed greater concern with regard to data analysis.

Dobyns (C) observed that it is difficult to know what data to rely on that can be used consistently and effectively. "There are mountains of data out there, but I think the biggest challenge is that it's really hard to draw the lines about what is real," she offered. Deming (C) added "There's so much data available that we're getting to the point where it could be analysis paralysis. What is the right metric? The strength is that the right data is available, the weakness is can we get everybody to agree what the right data is?"

In a similar but distinct concern about how data is analyzed, Wakshlag (M) observed a primary new concern for advertising measurement:

The challenge of bringing together two groups of people that have different traditions, the people from digital analytics versus people from media research. Their backgrounds are different. The guys who do digital analytics are generally really strong in mathematics and modelling. They can take data in any way, shape or form, start processing it, and come up with a decent way of looking at it, to know and understand what has happened. Also, if they're smart, they take that data and try to project it forward so they can start estimating with it, and predicting the future with it. And they're quite good at that. But what they don't have is an understanding of the quality of the data. It could be good data; it could be bad data. They treat it largely the same, while someone in media research is usually highly concerned with the quality of the data, as well as the analytics. So the media researcher is generally less sophisticated in mathematics and modeling, a less good data manipulator than somebody who's in digital analytics, but has a better and deeper understanding and knowledge of the quality of the data they're working with, and its limits.

Boehme (R) agreed with this sentiment and clearly expressed one of his main concerns with advertising measurement in today's environment: "The rampant adoption of data by non-researchers." He added:

The rise of the data scientist is important and necessary but data scientists are not by definition researchers, and the problem is interpreting the data. So you can have good data scientists who understand everything about the data set but have no idea about the

practical application of it."

Meanwhile, data volume was not reported as a concern from the scholarly participants.

*Trust.* Representatives from all participant groups acknowledged data reliability as a

challenge in today's advertising world. There was a virtual consensus that fraud and reported

delivery – especially from the digital side – were concerns.

Boehme (R) referred to the concern as a need for "transparency." Several agency

participants lamented the multiple issues with digital delivery reporting. Basham (A)

commented that "within digital there are just so many issues" and Mafredas observed "digital is

an absolute mess." Ivie (R) counted among his major concerns "things like invalid traffic and

fraud in digital."

From the client perspective, Hawkins (C) reported:

Some degree of distrust in the industry particularly in digital advertising, the impressions

that you're getting – that you're paying for – and click-through rates that are being

reported by the media companies that you're buying media from. Not that there is any

record of them being not reliable but just the unknown of, are those very accurate

numbers that you're paying for?

Similarly, Fielding (A) commented on the concerns of:

Bots or non-human traffic. I think that that's a very, very challenging subject area,

because I think there are certain elements of the industry that are not as committed as

others to find a solution for it because people are still making quite a bit of money out of

this.

*What should be measured?* Separately, the scholar participants suggested one area of concern that did not appear in the practitioner concerns.  This additional area of concern asks the question of what advertising research is actually measuring and whether the subject of the measurement in question aligns with what should (or could) be measured.

Thorson (S) suggested connecting the measurement of advertising to the goals of the campaign:

> I'd say the first problem for somebody that's putting their money into advertising, is to measure advertising in a way that's relevant to your campaign objective.  I see people measure stuff all the time, and it doesn't have anything to do with what they're trying to accomplish.

Hayes (S) observed that advertising is often measured against things that are not directly related to its capabilities.  He said:

> We often make our advertising goal [to be] sales, and that's how we measure the effectiveness of our advertising.  The problem with that is, communication can't drive sales.  Communication creates awareness.  It can drive preference.  It can help selection. We can't drive sales because we don't control the other parts of the four P's.

Duff (S) shared a story that explained this viewpoint:

> I went to a Marketing Data Science Symposium that Adobe was sponsoring last year, and I think that they do something like 40% of the Fortune 50 companies. They actually run the advertising through them, so they get all these metrics.  And they talked about their database, and how they want academics to be kind of looking at these variables.  They have 10,000 coded variables.  So looking at how we might think of these things as working or not working in various systems, and they're kind of asking about outcome variables then.  So you have all these coded

variables. What about, 'Do you have other outcome measures?' They said sales,

sales or click-through is always the outcome measure.

I said, 'Why would you have that for the advertising?' And they said, 'Well,

because this is what the brand managers want.' They want things you can put in a

nice neat package and say, 'Yes, this went up.' 'No, this went down.' But then to

me, that just means you're undervaluing your assets, because, of course, that's not

what advertising is good at directly. But it's easy to measure, and I think people

are falling into some of those traps of, 'Well, it gives you numbers and it's easy,

so this looks like something we'd want to use.'

The major concern with current advertising measurement from the scholar participants

was this disconnect of what is measured with advertising – which was not suggested as a concern

for the practitioners. This disconnect is evidence that the scholar-practitioner gap continues.

**Evolution of advertising and measurement.** Scholars and practitioners also tended to

see the future somewhat differently. Scholars identified five main areas of how advertising will

change: (1) increased pace of change, (2) reach and branding, (3) agreement on the basics, (4)

rise of data science, and (5) improved data. Meanwhile, practitioners collectively identified five

(mostly different) main areas of how advertising will change: (1) cross-platform emergence, (2)

consumption patterns, (3) need to improve copy, and (4) improved data, and (5) agreement on

the basics. Scholars and practitioners agreed only on two areas of evolution: improved data and

agreement on the basics. The scholar participants' areas of change are presented first, followed

by the practitioner participants' areas of change.

*Increased pace of change.* Schultz (S) argued that change is going to continue at an

accelerated pace:

I'm not worried about 10 years; I'm worried about three years.  Now, the problem is,

you're going to be talking to a lot of people who do not believe that, who believe it's

going to change maybe gradually that, 'I'll have time to adapt.  I'll have time to adjust,'

and historically they have, but I'm not sure they're going to have that in the future.

Sar (S) expressed that "all media platforms" are undergoing transformations and "we cannot

catch up with those that evolved and are changing every day."  For these scholars, the sheer

scope and pace of change is something that the advertising ecosystem is not able to keep up with.

*Reach and branding.*  For Romaniuk (S), the two biggest areas that need to change in

advertising were a focus on reach and a focus on branding.  She argued that it's important to

ensure messages are delivered "because we can only ever have an effect on the people that we're

reaching."  In the area of branding, she believes that it is necessary to consider and understand

how branding interacts with advertising because:

> No matter how you believe advertising works, it can't work if people don't know which
>
> brand is being advertised. That's one consistent thing I've found across people who have
>
> different philosophies in advertising that they can at least agree on.  But yet we still don't
>
> have those two fundamental components solved.

*Agreement on the basics.*  Similar to Romaniuk's search for agreement on "fundamental

concepts," Duff (S) proposed that those in the world of advertising need to consider what it is

that we want to measure.  She asked if we only want to know that we delivered an ad:

> Do we want to know that people received it?  What does that mean?  Then we
>
> need to start to ask, 'Okay, what are they receiving?  When?  Or what was
>
> delivered and when?  Do these things work separately?  Do they work together?
>
> When we say work, what does that mean?'  Now this is really sad, because

they're all such basic things, but as we move forward, and then you see things sort

of lurching forward separately, different media sort of will say, 'Oh look, we've

got a new way to measure this or do this.'

Note that Duff's observations here for the future of media and advertising are

similar to other scholars' concerns for the current landscape of measurement.

***Rise of data science.*** Hayes (S) saw the integration of data science and media research as

essential. He argued that agencies "need to understand what the data can allow, what it can

explain." He commented that they need data scientists and computer programmers because:

> They are the most equipped statistically to build in this new digital age. But what needs
>
> to happen from the academic point of view is, there need to be programs developed that
>
> will train communication people in data science, because the problem is, those data
>
> scientists can look at the numbers, but they have zero clue how to tell a story with those
>
> numbers for the brand. They don't understand communication enough to do that. They
>
> can tell you statistics, but they can't translate [them].

This is a theme that has surfaced multiple times from both the practitioner and scholar

communities. It appears that Hayes may be on the right track by developing and training media

researchers who also have data science skills.

***Improved data.*** Finally, Taneja (S) saw a future in which multi-source data would be

combined in ways that yield new insights:

> I think advertising measurement needs to make use of all the different capabilities of
>
> measuring that we have at our disposal, and we need to find creative ways to draw
>
> inferences from those different ways and use all these studies juxtaposed with one
>
> another to make sense of the bigger picture.

He suggested that data from multiple platforms, e.g., Twitter, Facebook, Nielsen, Google, and others could be combined using a variety of methods including statistical data fusion, for example, to generate newer insights.

On the other hand, professional practitioners in the field generally saw different evolutions of the advertising landscape in their predictions.

***Cross-platform emergence.*** Ivie (R) predicted that the industry will:

See cross-platform measurement evolve and emerge. We're far enough along the horizons of developing some of these tools where you're fairly certain they're going to come out. They're going to be used. I think it's going to change behavior. I think it's going to change advertising. So from a measurement standpoint, I think those are big, big directions.

While Ivie sees cross-platform measurement solutions emerging in some way; others are more specific. For example, Matarese (R) thought that impressions would emerge as the dominant cross-platform metric:

The KPI [key performance indicator] of measuring impressions and trying to normalize things to an impression, understanding that there are some nuances there in terms of what you're trying to accomplish by delivering your message. I think that is important because it's something that you can figure out ways of measuring for lots of different situations, even if it's how much traffic goes by the billboard.

***Consumption patterns.*** According to Gombas (R) "the reality is it's the consumer consumption changes that are going to really drive this." He believed that changes in consumer media usage would spur changes in the advertising industry. Winston (A) also commented that advertising measurement must evolve along with changes in media usage. Advertising "needs to better align with how people interact and spend their day," he said.  Many participants agreed with the contention that consumers will drive the changes in media based on their actions, usage, preferences, adoptions, and their purchase behaviors.

Garramone (M) agreed that advertising measurement would follow the consumer.  He predicts that "over the next three years, it's going to become fairly clear as to where things are heading from a consumption perspective."  Like Duff (S) above, he believed that "from a measurement standpoint, entities are going to take the leadership role.  It's going to be mostly sell-side entities who are going step in and say, 'This is how we suggest measuring all of our media.'"

Throckmorton (M) further agreed that consumer consumption is going to continue to change.  She observed, "at the end of the day, the only thing that's scarce is time, and people are fitting more consumption into that same 24 hours of the day."

Deming (C) observed that media would continue to evolve as well – from the consumer perspective, but also from the media perspective:

> I think everything's going to continue to be more one to one delivery, and I think the biggest change that's going to take place is how many players, frankly, are in the industry, and that's going to impact how fast the change takes shape. And by players I mean, who else is Facebook going to acquire?  Who else is Google going to acquire?  You're already starting to see the inroads of a handful of major players.

***Improve copy.***  Several industry participants suggested that the content of the ads themselves must evolve into something better.  For example, Meyer (A) suggested: "for starters, you kind of need to make ads that people would actually welcome."  Lal (M) agreed; she commented: "we need to actually start building better ad units."  D'Sylva (C) put it this way:

I'll tell you something that I always gravitate back to when I talk to people which, coming from a media guy, might seem almost blasphemous, which is, as a brand marketer, it still just comes down to the idea. When we have a great idea, as a brand, if executed extremely well creatively, we can carry it out across media, and do a fantastic job of getting it out there, it works.

Concerns about content that resonates with the target audience were echoed by others as well.

Johnson (C) concurred: "I think it's the right message, right time, right person." Zazula (R) argued that copy could be customized not only to people but to specific media delivery vehicles. She observed, "there is so much opportunity at the creative agencies to just create messages down to thinking about the device, thinking about the person, thinking about the delivery of message."

***Improved data.*** There appeared to be a general belief among the study participants that data will continue to improve and that it will be more usable instead of just in greater volume. Mafredas (A) was representative of this optimistic viewpoint: "As the data gets better and more refined, we'll be able to make better and smarter buys."

Hawkins (C) wanted a future in which users of the data have "accuracy of measuring what is being performed for the money that's being invested. So, absolute clarity and transparency and the numbers around on the digital of what's being delivered." He's asking for reliability and trustworthiness of the data.

Buchheim (R) saw more consistency and more specificity of advertising delivery data from a cross-platform perspective. He expressed it this way:

In a very privacy-compliant way, I would want to be able to understand who's seeing what ads and what content, and what time, on which device or platform. I think this is a little bit of the magic wand side, but if you could gain that

foundation, it would be a lot harder to continue the arguing about, 'Well, we don't

have the same way of counting over here that we do over there, and over there,

and over there.' And so even coming to agreement on standards would be a lot

easier, if you just said, 'Okay, we all have a common...' Let's get these

foundational elements out of the way, so that we can say, 'Okay, now, we have a

path.'

***Agreement on the basics.*** On the heels of Buccheim's comments, Dobyns (C) wanted a

future that follows the scientific method. She commented:

We just need more people to make decisions based on the data and be willing to test and

see what happens when they test based on data decisions instead of 'this is how we've

always done it' or 'this is what I'm most comfortable with' or 'this is what I know about.'

I think that really has to happen.

Wakshlag (M) argued that the advertising community needs to begin with the basics.

"People need to understand and agree that reach, frequency, and time are where you begin." He

also underscored that this agreement needs to happen in a cross-platform world. So, what

exactly are the basics? How do we get agreement on them? Who decides? And will there be

only one set of basics?

Boehme (R) also saw the future from a cross-platform perspective, but he thought that

there might be more than one answer. "I think standards will evolve, but I think they will be a

basket of currencies," he predicted. He argued that most of the data exists but "it's a question of

perfecting those systems for consistency and also other, I would say, pragmatic issues to make

sure that the data are affordable and accessible."

Scholars and practitioners agreed that the future must contain both improved data and industry agreement on the basics of cross-platform advertising measurement. However, each group generally thought three different areas would be more important to the evolution of the industry.

**Summary of Findings**

Study participants generally agreed that there were significantly more advantages (than disadvantages) to using impressions as a cross-platform advertising delivery measurement. Meanwhile, they also largely agreed that there remain significant challenges in creating, implementing, and adopting an impression-based measurement approach across media. Further, the study participants thought there were challenges in the current media ecosystem that still need to be addressed prior to the adoption of impression-based measurement. Finally, there were significantly more commonalities than differences between scholars and practitioners regarding the topic of the impression as a single media delivery measurement and its implementation – although there were a small number of significant differences between the groups.

Despite the findings from this particular study, research still shows a recognized disconnect between scholars and practitioners of advertising. One effort that might help make stronger connections between the two groups might be for scholars to pursue research that more closely aligns with the challenges faced by practitioners. For example, a general focus on improved measurement, and a specific focus cross-platform advertising measurement might prove helpful in crossing the divide between the two groups. Additional topic areas that might be amenable to helping build strong connections between the scholar and the practitioner communities include research on message delivery, especially those that tie back to ROI.

**Conclusion**

Chapter 4 reviewed the study approach, sample characteristics (including economic justifications for inclusion), and presented the findings for the four research questions, including categories developed from the data.

In chapter 5, these findings are analyzed and discussed in the context of the systems-based public relations process model to see how well the data set fits into that model. The findings will also be discussed with regard to the scholar-practitioner gap. Further, an advertising process model will be proposed. Finally, ideas will be suggested for next steps in the development and study of advertising impression measurement.

# Chapter 5

**Analysis, Conclusions, and Discussion**

This study set out to discover perspectives regarding the need for, nature of, and potential effectiveness of a cross-platform measure of advertising delivery -- specifically the impression -- by interviewing a diverse group of professionals from across the advertising ecosystem and evaluating their responses primarily through the lens of the systems-theory based public relations process model. The study found that these industry leaders and scholars largely agreed that there were significant advantages to using impressions as a cross-platform advertising delivery measurement. However, they also observed that there were important obstacles to moving forward with impression-based measurement. Finally, commonalities among scholars and practitioners were far more prevalent than differences between the two groups regarding the topic of advertising impression measurement.

This chapter is organized into four sections: (1) an analysis section, which considers the data in the context of the PR process model (described in Chapter 2), as well as supplemental qualitative analyses (from the participant data and study findings) to fill the gaps; (2) a discussion section, which (a) examines possible meanings of the findings and how they might be framed in order to understand their relevance better, (b) interprets the findings through the public relations process model, (c) considers differences between scholars and practitioners, and (d) proposes an advertising process model; (3) a limitations and future research section, which addresses study limitations and possible directions for future research related to the area of advertising impression measurement specifically and advertising and the public relations process model more generally; and, (4) a summary, which draws conclusions about the practical implications of the study and featured final remarks from the author.

As the commentary from the study participants is the essence of the data, and as limited extant research in the area of advertising delivery is available, the study will continue to draw liberally on participant quotes and observations.

**Analysis**

While participants in this study largely agreed that there were advantages to measuring cross-platform advertising delivery using impressions, they also expressed concern that there would be challenges for actual implementation of an impression-based measurement system. Although there were relevant differences between scholars and professionals in the advertising community, opinions were generally aligned between the two groups for most of the sub-topic areas identified.

**Analysis through the public relations process model.** As a reminder, the PR process model is a systems theory-based model that considers professional/organizational communication to be part of an on-going system. The study participants' commentary provided ample evidence that fit well into the PR process model – both in regard to the model subsystems and the dimensions of environmental supersystem. A brief review of that model is offered here as it presents a helpful conceptual guide for the ensuing analysis. (See Figure 1 for a visual depiction of the PR process model.)

*Three subsystems.* The model contains three sub-systems (organizational, communication, and target audience) that function as input, throughput, and output, respectively. Within each sub-system are specific elements:

1.      Organizational Subsystem – (input) contains organizational and public relations goals, management, resources, and strategy.

2.      Communication Subsystem – (transformation or throughput) contains the processes of message encoding and delivery.  This is where the beginning of message delivery measurement would be operationalized.

3.      Target Audience Subsystem – (output) contains the concepts of influence and/or maintenance/change of cognition/behavior.

The communication subsystem of the PR process model identifies message delivery.  The output of the communication subsystem is messages to which audiences may be exposed. "Physically, messages are tangible stimuli that can be perceived" (Long & Hazleton, 1987, p. 11).  If the messages can be perceived that presents an opportunity for them to be measured on a holistic basis – across multiple media and platforms.

Although the study participants were not directly asked about elements or concepts pertaining to the PR process model, their collective responses regarding the prospects and challenges of developing and implementing impression-based measurement can clearly be placed with the three sub-systems of the PR process model across the sample groups.

*Organizational subsystem.* Numerous comments (from the participants) aligned with the organizational subsystem of the PR process model.

- Fielding (A), Mafredas (A), Hayes (S), Thorson (S), Brami (M), Garramone, and Winston (A) all observed resources as a key component of advertising measurement.

- Lal (R), Schrag (M), Boehme (R), Thorson (S), Zazula, and Johnson (C) all highlighted strategic concerns as integral to advertising measurement.

Observations such as these (and many more) illustrate a strong goodness of fit between elements of advertising and the PR process model.  Numerous comments from the participants across the strata focused on goals, strategy, and resources – elements contained in the organizational subsystem of the PR process model.  As an organizational communication activity closely related to public relations, advertising similarly often emanates from organizations that have goals and strategies to achieve them in addition to a management structure that requires resources to operate.  The intention, purpose, and motivation for the communication activity originate in the organizational subsystem.  On the one hand, as well as the data fits (and it fits very well), the PR process model assumes that the source is always an organization.  Of course, this is the most likely scenario and that which occurs the vast majority of the time.  However, on the other hand, advertising might also be sourced from an individual, as in a political campaign. So while there must be a source, it might not always be an organization per se.

The findings indicated that advertising, as a messaging function (similar to public relations), contained similar organizational inputs likewise.  This alignment of the organizational subsystem factors across both PR and advertising indicated that the PR process model offered a lens through which to view and understand advertising that is supported by the data.

*Communication subsystem.*  Participant data showed strong goodness of fit for advertising in the PR process model in the communication subsystem as well.  Below are sample comments from the participants that aligned with the communication subsystem of the model.

- Zazula (R), Taneja (S), Matarese (R), Erichson (R), Moldenhauer (C), Garramone (M), Harb (M), Wakshlag (M), Meyer (A), Pearson (A), Basham (A), Fielding (A), and Mafredas (A) all commented on the importance of measurement.

- Buccheim (R) offered relevant thoughts on measurement that fit into the communication subsystem: "everything from the delivery of the ad, and counting that it actually was delivered, counting whether it was viewable or not, understanding engagement with the ad, or lack thereof."

- Romaniuk (S) noted the criticality of delivery measurement to audiences "because we can only ever have an effect on the people that we're reaching."

The formal message or messages are actually created here in the communication subsystem. Comments from the study participants focused on encoding or message creation and content as well as message output and measurement – elements that are all part of the communication subsystem of the PR process model. The findings showed that advertising, as a 'communication function' (similar to public relations), contains analogous communication elements. The communication subsystem is the section of the model that specifically calls out the delivery of the message. It is here in the process that measurement of impressions would begin (in 'delivery'). Further, multiple observations by study participants, including Lal (R), indicated that message content (aka creative) is an important and growing consideration for advertising. This consideration fits well with the 'encoding' of the message in the model. This alignment of the communication subsystem factors from the two similar subject areas of public relations and advertising suggested a justification that the PR process model presented a conceptualization to understand advertising better. However, one possible change for an advertising model might be to reposition the delivery of the message to a subsequent audience subsystem.

*Target audience subsystem.* Comments from the study participants showed an alignment of advertising with the target audience subsystem of the model as well. Here are a few examples:

- Fielding (A), Brami (M), Winston (A), Pearson (A), Wakshlag (M), Harb (M), Throckmorton (M), Schrag (C), Zazula (R), Hayes (S), Sar (S), Buchheim (R), and Johnson (C) all observed the impacts of messaging to the target audience.

- Jacobowitz (M) offered examples of maintenance or change in cognitions/attitudes/behaviors, including "perception, retention, recall."

- Schultz (S) commented that there are "two ways of looking at advertising measurement. Are you looking at measuring attitudes or are you looking at measuring behaviors?"

These observations from the study participants (and others) addressed topics of influence and audience cognitions or behaviors (effects) – elements represented in the target audience subsystem of the PR process model. It is in the target audience subsystem stage of the process that the measurement of delivery (e.g., impressions) culminates. Further, it is in the target audience that virtually all impactful measurement (and tactical impacts) occur. For advertising, there would be a host of potential metrics, including not only delivery but also measures of attitudes, brand, intent to purchase, and, potentially, sales. This measurement feeds into to the feedback loop of the advertising (PR) process and is the end goal of advertising: to maintain or change either cognitions (attitudes, beliefs, preferences) or behaviors (purchasing behavior, voting, etc.). It is important to reiterate that the target audience subsystem is where most measurement actually occurs. Delivery measurement (i.e., impressions) must occur before psychologically-based measurements.

Here again, the findings showed that advertising contains target audience elements that are similar to those in public relations. This concurrence of the target audience subsystem factors from the two similar subject areas (advertising and PR) strongly support the argument that the PR process model could prove useful in helping to analyze and understand advertising.

Generally, the findings in this study indicated an extremely strong support for, and goodness of fit with, the three sub-systems of the PR process model. These connections are important because they provided ample evidence that the model could help conceptualize advertising as a process that might be better understood in the framework of a systems theory approach.

*Environmental supersystem.* In the PR process model, the three sub-systems exist inside a larger environmental supersystem that is composed of five overlapping, interacting dimensions of the environment: (1) political/legal, (2) economic, (3) competitive, (4) technological, and (5) social. Each dimension addresses factors that influence the process of organizational communication:

1. Political/legal – This dimension is characterized by rules which govern organizational conduct and enforcement, including legislation and judicial processes.

2. Economic – This dimension includes financial and monetary resources and constraints.

3. Competitive – The competitive dimension includes an array of competitors, both internal to, and external to the industry.

4. Technological – This dimension includes technology, devices, and/or knowledge systems (software) impacting the organization.

5. Social – Finally, the social dimension includes the publics and stakeholders of the organization.

Comments from the study participants also integrated well with all five of the environmental dimensions of the PR process model. Further, the comments relating to the environmental dimensions represented an acknowledgment of these dimensions across the study participant segments. Collectively, they demonstrated that representatives of the advertising measurement industry – and its subparts (when considering the possibilities of an impression-based measurement approach) – are influenced in specific ways by the five factors of the environmental supersystem that have been included in the PR process model.

*Political/Legal Dimension.* Below are sample comments from the participants that support the political/legal dimension of the model.

- Privacy was the most oft-cited political/legal area of concern. A few examples include: Basham (A) commented: "You have to weigh measurement with privacy." Dobyns (C) prognosticated that "privacy is going to get even more important." Meanwhile, Duff (S) noted "privacy, and ethical concerns." Boehme (R) also discussed the importance of such concerns: "Now we can see how advertising can be matched to specific purchasing in a privacy compliant manner."

- Wakshlag (M), Erichson (R), Danaher (S), and others acknowledged additional political and/or legal concerns.

The political/legal dimension of the PR Process model deals with laws, rules, regulations, and enforcement; the comments from the study participants above represented these elements in abundance. Concerns about privacy in a media environment that is growing more and more personal (of a social nature utilizing one-to-one transmission/reception with personally identifiable information) continue to be of relevance and will likely only increase. How data and issues of privacy are addressed have already attracted the attention of legislatures and corporate lobbyists. The 'walled gardens' of major digital entities, such as Apple, Facebook, and others that contain reams of personal information are likely to become subject to increasing legal scrutiny. Questions of ownership – and access – regarding that collective data are relevant. Laws and enforcement will continue to have a significant and growing impact on media and, as a result, on advertising.

Conceptualizing the various legal and political concerns from the participants as one of several environmental dimensions emphasizes the interconnectedness of important factors relevant to advertising as well as public relations.

*Economic Dimension.* The participants' comments support and align with the economic dimension of the PR process model.

- Fielding (A), Winston (A), Schultz (S), Garramone (M) and others argued that consideration of economic issues is essential to advertising.

In a similar vein, more than half the participants brought up relative valuation as an important economic metric (almost exclusively from the practitioner segments). More than a quarter of the participants brought up budgets as a major economic factor. Further, Lal (M), Schrag (C), Boehme (R) and others cited return-on-investment (ROI) as a critical metric for advertising.

Meanwhile, Kahn (A), Winston (A), Meyer (A), Deming (C), Thorson (S), Romaniuk (S), Hayes (S) and others brought up concerns about the cost-prohibitive nature of research and the impact of high prices. Financial considerations are extremely relevant to advertising. As a business effort, concerns of cost, investment, return and the bottom line are key factors for advertising. How the resources are distributed across multiple media options for advertising efforts are essentially resource allocation decisions. It is important that such decisions are informed by intelligent data and analyses. The use of AIM as a cross-platform measurement could help improve the inputs to those decisions.

The economic dimension of the PR process model deals with resources (budgets) and costs; the comments from the study participants showed further goodness of fit with these elements demonstrating support for using the PR process model for advertising. Understanding economic concerns from the participants as one of several environmental dimensions emphasized that there were multiple relevant dimensions that can be considered as part of the overall system.

*Competitive Dimension.* Competition is an important element in a dynamic media environment in which media are competing for advertising dollars but which also represents competitive organizations trying to sell products and ideas through advertising with those media. Below are sample comments from the participants that support the competitive dimension of the model:

- Fielding (A) cited competitive concerns among major media as an impediment to data sharing and improved advertising measurement.
- Pearson (A), Wakshlag (M), Throckmorton (M), Salisch (M), Hawkins (C), Zazula (M), Taneja (S), Schrag (C), Erichson (R), and Boehme (R) all discussed the competitive nature of media and advertising.

By its very nature, advertising helps companies respond to competitive threats – or initiates them. Boehme (R) argued that advertising helps companies "exploit competitive advantages." Further, media outlets themselves are competing with each other to deliver messages for advertising organizations and to extract revenue from that effort. As media continue to expand, measurement across the various media options will continue to grow as a need. But competitive concerns go beyond just the direct competition for exposures and revenue; they also include competitive aspects in employee recruitment and even considerations in the digital arena for topics such as access to (ownership of?) limited spectrum and bandwidth.

The competitive dimension of the PR Process model addresses competing organizations and competitive environments; observations from the study participants recognized these elements.  Viewing these concerns individually as related to each other, and collectively as one of several environmental dimensions, allowed them to be appreciated as sets of concerns that can and do impact on each other.

*Technological Dimension.*  Commentary from the participants that support the technological dimension of the model came from all five of the strata.

- Jacobowitz (M) observed the importance of technology for data collection and management.

- Garramone (M) spoke about the importance of technology infrastructure in advertising.

- Winston (A) observed that media technology has begun a shift from centralized sourcing to de-centralized control of content (as in the case of social media, user-generated content, and streaming services) and now "control of the message, control of the media…is now in the hands of the consumer or the audience."

- Many others, including Fielding (A), Pearson (A), Wakshlag (M), Lal (M), Salisch (M), Gombas (R),  Boehme (R), Matarese (R) and Ivie (R) observed the highly impactful nature of technology to advertising.

Hayes (S) suggested that new technologies offer opportunities for scholars and practitioners to work together.  This might present one avenue to explore the scholar-practitioner gap.

Technology in the dynamic media environment has enormous impacts on the media that people consume, the data that is collected by media researchers, and on how resources are allocated across the advertising ecosystem.  There is a dichotomy in that many believe that technology and new data will somehow magically improve the measurement process; meanwhile most also believe that the world of media and advertising will continue to grow increasingly complicated.  The 'complication factor' is also relevant to concerns for cross-platform advertising as the advances in technology are not likely to be evenly distributed across media types and platforms.

"Shiny, new objects" are the embodiment of technological advancements.  Wakshlag (M), Throckmorton (M), and Zazula (R) all expressed the risks that the shiny, new technologies present.  Taneja observed that it is important to make sense "of how people actually deal with all these different platforms and technologies."  The reality is that technology is likely not going to slow down, so media and advertising researchers must continue to recognize and embrace the changes as part of their models.  Further, technology and economic issues can overlap when it comes to access to technology – not everyone can afford the new iPad or the latest iPhone or even the unlimited mobile data plans that often power them.  The so-called digital divide – where some consumers do not have internet access in their homes – is an example of the crossover of technology and financial concerns.  This is but one example of the inter-connectedness of the advertising process.

Technology is also caught up in a seemingly never-ending cycle of advancements and counterstrikes to defeat (and circumvent) bot traffic and fraud in digital ad measurement.

The technological dimension of the PR Process model deals with advancements and systems; the observations from the study participants addressed these elements well.  The study participants recognized that technological advancements offer both promise and risk. Considering technological factors as elements that affect the advertising system emphasizes that these concerns exist as an integral part of the overall process in the environmental supersystem.

*Social Dimension.* The social dimension of the environment was another area in which the participant data provided significant alignment to the model. Below are sample comments from the participants that support the social dimension of the model.

- Virtually every participant commented on the impact of social media. Facebook, Twitter, Instagram, and a host of other 'social media' are a hugely impactful set of technologies that have profoundly impacted the social environment.

- Meyer (A), Wakshlag (S), Jacobowitz (M), Dobyns (C), Ivie (R), Matarese (R), and Zazula all discussed topic directly connected to the social dimension of the model, including stakeholders, consumer behavior, social activism, social change, engagement and other related areas.

There are multiple areas in which advertising concerns suggested by the participants relate to the social dimension of the environment. For example, consuming media is often a social activity and, in some cases, even leads to relationships such as those studied in parasocial interaction. The rise of social media has further integrated media (and in some ways, advertising) into the social fabric of our increasingly digital culture. Many people now communicate as much with social media (often ad-supported) as they do in other, more traditional fashions. Millions use Instagram, Snapchat, etc. to message, eschewing SMS texting or even the good, old-fashioned telephone call – to say nothing of the ancient arts of face-to-face conversation or public speaking. Further, social activism is an area that has begun to make more use of advertising; sometimes to deliver messages, but also, according to Dobyns (C), to pressure advertisers to avoid supporting objectionable content. Ivie (R) observed, "our society relies a lot on advertising to not only conduct commerce, but effectuate social change."

Comments from the study participants aligned with the social dimension of the PR Process model which addresses group and individual concerns and how they are influenced by opinion leaders and other groups. The study supported the contention that advertising is social in nature and has tentacles reaching into all manner of social areas. Considering social factors as one of several dimensions that are part of an advertising process offered utility to help understand advertising in ways that are interconnected and related, as the PR process model illustrates.

The data demonstrated firm support for, and goodness of fit with, the five dimensions of the PR process model. Overall, the findings indicated that advertising process and related concerns mesh well with the structure of the PR process model, including both the three subsystems and the five environmental dimensions. Collectively, the findings offered a way to conceptualize advertising: as a process that is part of a complex, inter-related system. The alignment of advertising to the multiple elements of the model supported viewing advertising through the lens of a systems meta-theoretical perspective. Thus, the PR process model helped to organize the perspectives expressed by a diverse group of advertising experts in regard to their views of advertising impression measurement. Using this conceptualization enhanced the understanding of advertising as a process that 1) has specific inputs, throughputs, and outputs, and 2) effects and is affected by dimensions of the environment.

**Analysis further mapping study data to the public relations process model.** As noted earlier, there is a significant lack of scholarship on the topic of advertising delivery. Meanwhile, Rose (2012) identified messaging as a "process" (p. 564) further supporting the claim that it can be considered from a systems perspective. A host of researchers have examined similar

organizational phenomena from a systems perspective. While Long and Hazleton (1987) include

message encoding and delivery as key parts of the PR process model, those aspects of the

process are described as "technical/administrative" and are not explored in great depth.

However, they did identify the messages (assumed to be delivered) as "communication

subsystem outputs… to which audiences are exposed" (p. 11). In addition, it was shown in

previous sections that the results of this study could be aligned with all of the major components

of the model.

In these previous sections, some of the study findings and related individual comments

from the study participants were mapped to fit into the structure of the PR process model. In this

next section, various categories from the findings derived from the analysis of data pertaining

specifically to research questions 2 and 3 were evaluated regarding how well or not they align

with, or can be further understood, using the PR process model.

According to the study participants, there were eight challenges for impression-based

measurement (results that addressed RQ2): (1) vested interests, (2) standards, (3) comparison, (4)

data access, (5) definition of impression, (6) complexity of media environment, (7) relative

valuations, and (8) cost. How do each of these relate to the PR Process model?

1. *Vested interests* – With potential economic impact and competitive repercussions,

   vested interests aligned with the financial and competitive dimensions of the

   environment.

2. *Standards* – Standards stemmed from the competitive dimension and potentially

   from the legal dimension of the environment (depending on the degree of

   formality of the standards). In addition, there were measurement implications of standards within the target audience subsystem. However, it should be noted that the model did not address standards per se.

3. *Comparison* – Comparison across media with regard to delivery is generally a more detailed concept than those addressed by the PR process model. However, the model does discuss media/channel selection and factors that influence the selection. Further, an argument could be made that the competitive dimension of the environment considers comparative concerns. Although a detailed multi-media comparison construct is a missing component when this model is applied to the impression-based measurement context that was the focus of this study, the model could accommodate this challenge.

4. *Data Access* – Access to data is another area not covered explicitly by the PR process model. The PR Process model (along with most researchers who have conducted studies relative to this topic) seemed to assume that data would be available as part of the evaluation.

5. *Definition of Impression* – As discussed above, a precise, operational definition of a cross-platform impression currently eludes the industry. Such a definition is another area that is more detailed than the PR process model currently delineates for exploration. However, the model does indicate that the organizational subsystem (transformation section) is where message delivery exists. Subsequently, the model provides a conceptual basis for measurement of the messages in the target audience subsystem. So there might be a logical place in which to incorporate a metric of this nature into the model.

6. *Complexity of Media Environment* – As a relatively static conceptualization that

focuses more on the messages themselves, their general flow, and their impact –
instead of the possible, specific delivery methods, the PR process model does not
address complexity of media environment.

7. *Relative Valuations* – Differential valuation of media vehicles is another area that
   is not addressed in the PR process model.

8. *Cost* – Cost of media and measurement is addressed in the model generally along
   with other factors.  Long & Hazleton (1984) observed that "factors affecting
   media selection include the environment, function the medium performs for the
   audience, cost, content limitations, speed, control, and level of audience
   involvement" (p. 11).  However, cost is not specifically explored in detail.

The vast majority of the challenges for impression-based measurement that were
described by the study participants as it related to RQ2 are not reflected in, nor addressed by, the
PR process model.  In fact, none of the challenges suggested by the participants is addressed by
the model directly, although a small number of them (cost and comparison) is addressed
indirectly.

Next, seven additional themes or considerations that emerged from the analysis of the
study participants' collective responses (and which addressed RQ3) can be considered in light of
the PR process model and its various components.  These themes reported in Chapter 4 were (1)
the enormity of the task at hand (Scale), (2) the rise of data science and its integration into the
marketing world (Data Science vs. Media & Marketing), (3) the changes in media and the media
ecosystem (Media Evolution), (4) the problem of data kept behind 'firewalls' away from other
media and advertisers (Walled Garden), (5) making better, more relevant content for advertising
messages (Creative), (6) non-human traffic or false reporting of advertising delivery (Fraud), and

(7) distraction due to new developments (Bright, Shiny, New Things).  Next, each of these additional considerations was examined as to its potential fit into the model.

1. *Scale* – Concerns about the massive scale of data in today's multimedia messaging world were not anticipated, and therefore not addressed, by the PR process model.

2. *Data Science vs. Media & Marketing* – Just as the enormous increase in scale was not foreseen by the model, neither was the somewhat antagonistic relationship of data science vs. media and marketing professionals that have evolved from the virtual explosion of media.

3. *Media Evolution* – Yet again, the incredible evolution of media was not predicted by the model.

4. *Walled Garden* – The lack of data sharing – largely created by self-contained media systems – is another downstream impact of media evolution and scale that was not predicted by the model.

5. *Creative* – Unlike most of the other considerations, the PR process model does address the creative content of messages.  It considers solution character of the message and audience analysis aspects in the formulation of the message in the output section of the organizational subsystem.  Further, the model addresses the actual creation of the message (aka encoding) in the communication subsystem – both in the creation of the message 'program' (input section) and in the encoding of the message itself (transformation section).

6. *Fraud* – Primarily seen as a downstream impact of the rise of digital advertising, fraud was not anticipated by the model.

7. *Bright, Shiny, New Things* – The chance for distraction from new technologies is another concept that was not addressed specifically by the PR process model. However, it should be noted that 'bright, shiny, new things' could be interpreted as impacts from the technological dimension of the model's environmental supersystem.

In general, the additional considerations observed for cross-platform impression measurement are virtually unaddressed by the public relations process model. In fact, only two of the further challenges suggested by the participants (creative content and bright, shiny, new things) were addressed specifically by the model. However, the systems-based underpinnings of the model could certainly accommodate most, if not all of these considerations.

The commentary from the study participants fit the PR process model well at a high level, but the additional considerations and challenges offered by the group of practitioners and scholars were not explained specifically by the model. However, the flexibility of the model could be utilized to capture the challenges and considerations.

**Discussion**

This section further discusses and explains the results of the study, drawing conclusions based on them and considers the implications they may have for practitioners and scholars interested in this area of practice and study.

**Review of research questions and findings.** The participants shared broad agreement that the benefits of an impression-based advertising measurement (AIM) approach far outweighed potential negatives. However, the participants also expressed significant concerns regarding the challenges associated with the operationalization of AIM approach for measuring advertising delivery across media. The responses indicate that there is a strong case to be made for the impression as cross-platform media measurement from multiple perspectives across the advertising community.

The participants noted eight challenges to creating, implementing, and adopting an impression-based measurement approach across multiple media.  The eight categories included vested interests, standards, comparison, data access, definitions, complexity of media environment, relative valuations, and cost.  These are obstacles that the participants believe will hinder the adoption and usage of impression as a cross-platform media metric.

The participants further suggested seven additional areas that need to be addressed regarding impression measurement in today's dynamic media environment.  The seven are scale; data science vs. media & marketing; media evolution; walled garden; creative; fraud; and bright, shiny, new things.  These issues are ones that the participants believe are relevant in both the current media environment and beyond.  These considerations are relevant to multiple factors of impression/delivery measurement for advertising.

**Evaluation of data relative to public relations process model.**  As noted in earlier chapters, topics of cross-platform advertising delivery measures have been minimally addressed.  One reason is that the theories most often applied to advertising and its effects generally approach the subject from a psychological perspective (i.e., considering the impact and interpretation of messages within the recipient's mind).  Such theories (e.g., hierarchy of effects models) examine advertising after the message has been delivered by contemplating various internal effects of messaging (McGuire, 1961; Petty & Cacioppo, 1984; Lavidge & Steiner, 2000; Kim, Kayes, Avant, & Reid, 2014).  Therefore, measurement of message delivery (from these theoretical viewpoints) is not a relevant factor.  These approaches also tend to consider messaging on a micro (or individual) perspective.  Therefore, they merely assume that the delivery of the message has occurred.  Further, the few cross-platform studies that have been undertaken contain two important disadvantages: 1) they do not look at delivery, and 2) they usually look at a small number of media (Shen, 2002; Naik & Raman, 2003; Chang & Thorson, 2004; McGrath, 2005; Schultz, Block, and Raman, 2009; Tudor, 2009; Yunjae, Leckenby & Eakin, 2011; Danaher and Dagger, 2013).

More generally, the field of advertising lacks broad conceptualizations that can be open to multiple interpretations and varied applications that accommodate the vast array of advertising types and specialties.  This theoretical void is a virtual, invisible chasm that appears to be underpinned by pre-occupation with psychologically-based theories of persuasion and attitude change.  For the field to continue to develop, theoretic approaches to advertising need to expand.  One way in which that expansion might be operationalized is by utilizing a meta-theoretic approach such as systems theory, and a specific example of that approach that appears helpful is the public relations process model.  As this study demonstrated, there is a strong linkage between the concepts of the PR process model and concepts of advertising.  For the PR process model to evolve into a more useful 'advertising' process model, it would be necessary for the public relations process model to be modified in at least four ways.

First, the model needs to be retrofitted into a true advertising (instead of public relations) process model.  This would likely involve adding to the structure to incorporate the advertising agency model and media to a greater degree.  Second, the model must be updated to incorporate the realities of today's complex media environment.  Changes in this area would require adjustments to recognize the current dynamic media environment, including the growing plethora of digital or Internet-based media options (such as social media).  Third, the PR process model must be further developed to incorporate sufficient detail and specificity to accommodate important elements such as measurement delivery. Meaningful concepts to include from this perspective include reach, frequency, and duration of message exposure in addition to definitional elements such as the impression and CPM, but also possibly CPP, etc. as appropriate. Fourth, an 'advertising' process model would need to include message/campaign evaluation factors such as relative valuation of media vehicles and concepts such as advertising effects, including components such as ROI. Further, the model would need to utilize the systems approach to delve into fuller descriptions applied to advertising concerns.

In addition, a meta-theoretic approach to the study of advertising offers additional benefits beyond the 'practical' goodness of fit (or appropriateness) of the conceptualization and openness to new ideas and inputs. It also brings heuristic value because its meta-theoretic approach can accommodate additional theory-building. Further an 'advertising process model' is relatively parsimonious. It is conceptually simple enough to fit on a single page but offers a virtually infinite ability to drill down or expand upward and outward. Finally, this approach is supported by the face validity generated from the findings of the present study.

This study was primarily interested in the exposure of messages to audiences (impressions) and the measurement of that exposure. The collective results gained from interviews with a wide variety of professionals and scholars with expertise regarding advertising measurement today offer many new insights regarding the need for and challenges in developing and applying a meaningful cross-platform messaged delivery measurement or system. As shown earlier in this chapter, the PR process model seems to offer a valuable perspective through which to examine advertising management systems — and impression-based measurement systems in particular. It offers potential as a guide in explaining the process involved in this case because many of the results of this study seemed to fit relatively neatly into the model. However, the analysis also served to identify particular ways the model fell short in explaining and guiding the

development and application of impression-based measurement systems in today's constantly

changing, complex, digital multi-media environment.  In the following section, several reasons

for the shortfalls are presented.

***Four possible reasons for the gaps.***  One reason that the model has gaps is that it has not

been developed with enough detail to get down too many of the specific needs for the present

application.  To be fair, the model is a general conceptualization; meanwhile, some of the

concerns surfaced from the participants regarding message delivery and measurement are quite

specific and detailed in nature.  While the model correlates with much of the commentary of the

individual participants and study findings in terms of structure, it does not address some of the

group concerns addressing detailed message delivery and measurement for impressions.

A second important reason the model does not address many of the study participants'

concerns is that the model was originally designed to represent public relations and not

advertising per se.  However, as discussed earlier, both of those functions are closely related to

the marketing scheme.  They both deal with organizational communication.  Thorson and

Rodgers (2012) claim that advertising is a form of communication.  Similarly, Long and

Hazleton (1987) argue that public relations are a communication function.  As discussed

previously, both advertising and public relations are included in the promotion aspect of

marketing and are therefore closely related as organizational communication concepts.  So there

is a theoretical justification for examining these concepts in a similar vein.

Yet a third potential reason that the model is not sufficient for today's media environment

is that it simply did not anticipate the massive changes and expansion in the media and delivery

environment that have occurred in the past three decades.  However, it should be noted that the

GST approach, by its nature, is open to environmental impacts, including the explosion of technological impacts that have occurred in the time since the model was developed. Perhaps all that is needed would be an interpretive update to bring the model up to contemporary standards.

A fourth possible reason that the model lacks in some areas has to do with the difference between academic concept and functional implementation. Often, academic concepts must be broad enough to cover entire categories of study. Theories are designed to be applied across large swaths of data. According to Long & Hazleton (1984), "systems theory is a structure of science, i.e., it has no substance by itself and must be applied. Systems analyses are abstract. They deal with symbols that stand for aspects of real objects and interrelationships" (p. 13). Disconnects such as this may offer a conceivable explanation for why, according to Li (2012), "the gap in advertising research between academia and the industry" stubbornly persists (p. 550). Yet, the findings in this study indicate that the PR process model does provide a defensible and potentially valuable starting point to be applied to advertising measurement.

***Next steps for advertising impression measurement and associated theory development.*** According to the participants of this study, the impression offers a useful avenue to explore for cross-platform media advertising delivery. The findings of this study agree with both Smit and Neijens (2011) and Shen (2002) who have also recommended using impression measurement as a cross-media measurement concept. According to Cannon (2012), "the integrative nature of modern media planning" is an important aspect of media evaluation and quantitative judgment should be used in that process (p. 333). As Taylor et al. (2013) observed, marketers are deficient in the information they require to make intelligent media decisions in today's complicated, multimedia environment. In the view of the participants of this study, impression-based measurement might help address some of these deficiencies.

Part of the challenge seems to lie in that persistent disconnect between scholars of advertising and practitioners in the field (although this study found that the two groups agreed more often than not).  Faber, Duff, & Nan (2012) suggested that more research into advertising from an applied perspective is needed.  Krugman and Hayes (2012) argue that despite a lack of formal theories of advertising, it is important "to continually examine, understand, and explain how the field operates to advance both knowledge and practice" (p. 435).

Clearly, the PR process model, as applied in this particular study, has a compelling fit with the basic environmental concerns, structure, and concepts of advertising.  However, the model also lacks the structural specificity to be applied to advertising delivery in a detailed and meaningful manner.

The next section looks at the scholar-practitioner gap as observed by the study participants in greater detail.

**Differences between scholars and practitioners.**  As the results of this study revealed in chapter 4, there were both commonalities and differences among practitioner and scholar views about advertising impression measurement.  Five primary areas were recognized in which the commonalities and differences between practitioners (who conduct advertising activities) versus academics (who study the topic) showed significant relevance.  They are discussed further here:

***Why advertising is measured.***  Scholars and practitioners agreed that measuring advertising is important, but their rationale for that measurement was different.  Scholars focused on assessment of activities, output, and effectiveness.  Meanwhile, practitioner reasons for measuring advertising were ROI, wise spending, optimization, and transactional value.  Scholars are generally concerned with what can be learned and what can be predicted.  On the other hand, practitioners are far more focused on measures of relative value, such as ROI and how to optimize advertising expenditures versus results. While scholars are still searching for a definition of advertising results, practitioners are measuring what they have at their disposal. It would seem that the practitioners have a bias toward action. This area represents both some alignment but also a divergence between the two groups. This particular concept could serve as a metaphor for the scholar-practitioner gap: agreement that measurement is important but disagreement on what should be measured and why.

*Using impressions as a cross-platform metric.* There was broad agreement from both scholars and practitioners as to the benefits of an impression-based measurement approach for advertising. Meanwhile, few disadvantages were suggested to using impressions as a cross-platform media metric, but those few were expressed by both scholars and practitioners. The findings indicate significant agreement exists between the two groups with regard to advertising impression measurement. These areas of agreement are evidence that there exist opportunities to close the scholar-practitioner gap.

*Challenges for impression-based measurement.* Both practitioners and scholars tended to agree on six out of eight of the challenges to impression-based measurement. Only two challenges to impression measurement (standards and comparability) were recognized by practitioners alone. While both groups seemed to have a similar understanding of the challenges that would be faced with an impression-based measurement approach, practitioners recognized more challenges. Looking at the nature of the two additional challenges presented by the practitioners, it makes sense that both of them (standards and comparability) are highly implementational in nature (things that practitioners would be highly interested in). In essence, practitioners are concerned with these challenges because they have to be. Without such specifics, an impression-based approach could not be put into actual practice. The logic is simple: scholars are free to theorize, but if practitioners cannot operationalize a concept, it has little value to them. The opportunity going forward would be to figure out how to connect the two groups in order to address some of the challenge areas in which they agree.

***Current concerns with advertising measurement.*** The major concern with current advertising measurement indicated by the scholar participants was a disconnect of what is actually measured with advertising – which was not an important concern for the practitioners. This area, more than any other, seemed to crystallize the basis for differing viewpoints between practitioners and scholars. Similar to the first difference above (*Why advertising is measured*), scholars are much more focused on defining what is actually being measured. At the same time, practitioners have little use (or time, or resources) to consider potential measures that cannot be implemented or that are difficult to report. In general, practitioners measure two things: delivery (impressions, ratings, etc.) and sales-related metrics (revenue, volume). Some scholars argue that sales, in particular, is not an appropriate metric for advertising and therein lies another reason for the scholar-practitioner gap. It's logical that, because the scholar-practitioner gap exists in the current environment, current concerns would reflect the gap.

***Evolution of advertising and measurement.*** As Table 2 reveals, both scholars and practitioners agreed that the future must contain both improved data and industry agreement on the basics of cross-platform advertising measurement. However, each group also predicted three divergent areas would be more important to the evolution of the advertising measurement.

Focusing on the differences that each group places on the future needs of the industry, it is clear that the priorities vary depending on the lens one is using. It could be argued that the concepts surfaced as priorities from the scholars (data science, branding, and pace of change) are broader and somewhat more esoteric – and definitely less 'applied.' This is not to say that these

**Table 2**

*Advertising Change Predicted by Segment*

| Scholar | | Practitioner |
|---|---|---|
| improved data | *same* | improved data |
| agreement on the basics | *same* | agreement on the basics |
| **rise of data science** | ***different*** | **consumption patterns** |
| **reach and branding** | ***different*** | **need to improve copy** |
| **increased pace of change** | ***different*** | **cross-platform emergence** |

concepts are not important; they are – and many were discussed by practitioner participants but not as keys for industry evolution.  On the other side of the coin, the concepts arising as priorities from the practitioners are more concerned with 'nuts and bolts' of how to follow the consumer (consumption patterns), how to make ads work better (improving copy), and how to deal with the explosion of media and the need to integrate it (cross-platform emergence).  Such concerns are definitely more 'applied' in nature.  It's possible that examining the areas of agreement in greater depth might reveal that they are not necessarily in complete agreement.  For example, while all of the participant groups wanted more data, the practitioners were much more concerned about how to get the data and if it would be reliable; meanwhile, the scholars were more concerned with what data would be available.  Further, the two participant groups might not agree as to what the 'basics' actually are.

While the results of this study indicated significant agreement in many areas of advertising measurement, there remain gaps between scholars and practitioners.  According to Faber, Duff, & Nan (2012) advertising is a 'variable' field (like journalism and political science -

- not a 'level' field, such as psychology or sociology).  Variable fields explore specific

phenomenon and therefore – perhaps – they may require more specific (applied) research with

regard to theory development.  Such research efforts might serve as a start to help bridge the gap

between scholars and practitioners.

**Reciprocity.**  It is important to consider the interplay between the practical and scholarly

communities.  Despite the scholar-practitioner gap, connections abound in both directions.  One

example of this interconnectivity is how research on the gap – and research utilizing efforts to

address the gap – might help to minimize it.  Another example of reciprocity could be the

challenges to cross-platform measurement observed by practitioners that could serve as potential

research topics for scholars.

**An advertising process model.**  Although not the purpose of this study, the logical next

step would be to propose an initial version of an advertising process model based on the findings

of the study.  As with any model, there are a set of assumptions that should be clearly identified.

First, the advertising process model (APM) considers advertising to be a process from the meta-

theoretical perspective of GST.  Second, advertising is considered to be an organizational

communication activity.  Scholars agree that advertising is a form of communication (Stern,

1994; Thorson and Rodgers, 2012).  Third, this model also agrees with Thorson and Rodgers

(2012) that advertising exists under the larger concept of marketing.  Fourth, unlike many

theoretical approaches to advertising, the APM does not take a purely psychological approach to

advertising (although the model does allow for psychological approaches in the audience

subsystem).  It approaches the subject from a more holistic and objective viewpoint that

incorporates both sociological and psychological perspectives.  Fifth, the APM utilizes the

definition of advertising laid out early in this study.

***Describing the APM.*** The APM is modeled after the approach used by the PR process

model. As such, it incorporates the relevant applications of the study data that fit so well with

that model. One can clearly see the obvious high-level similarities of an advertising process

model to the PR process model. However, the APM seeks to modify the approach to fit

advertising's specific needs, strategies, goals, inputs, terminology, and measurement concerns in

today's dynamic media environment more fully. In addition, the APM utilizes elements similar

to those recognized by Nan and Faber (2004) for communication-based advertising theoretical

constructs, including source, message, media, reception, and feedback.

Many advertising models previously developed consider only narrow slices or specific

applications of advertising. Baker and Lutz (2000) suggested the relevance-accessibility model

of advertising that focused on brand choice; Waller (2005) proposed a model that dealt with

controversial advertising; Ha and McCann (2008) created a model of advertising clutter; and

Wang and Sun (2010) produced an advertising model that addressed just online advertising.

Beyond these specific foci, the APM is needed to represent the overall, conceptual and

applied advertising process, including all facets of the practice and scholarly research. Because

the APM conceptualizes advertising at a broad level, it has the ability to incorporate all of the

various types and kinds of advertising, including commercial advertising, political advertising,

advertising to children, and any other types of advertising. While all may be relevant and of

specific importance to those that practice and study those particular incarnations of advertising,

they can all be considered within the APM. The APM is composed of an environmental

supersystem and three subsystems. (See Figure 3.) The environmental supersystem includes a

multi-dimensional environment that has five dimensions: Political/legal, economic, competitive,

technological, and social. These are described above and are remarkably aligned to those same dimensions of the PR process model for reasons already reviewed.  As such, they will not be discussed in further detail here.

However, the three subsystems differ from the PR process model and will, therefore, be described in greater detail (although many of the concepts are highly similar).  As indicated above, systems are composed of subsystems and are part of supersystems.  So, just as the source-communication-audience process contains an input-throughput-output for the overall advertising process, each of the subsystems is composed of its own input-throughput-output components.



*Advertising Process Model*

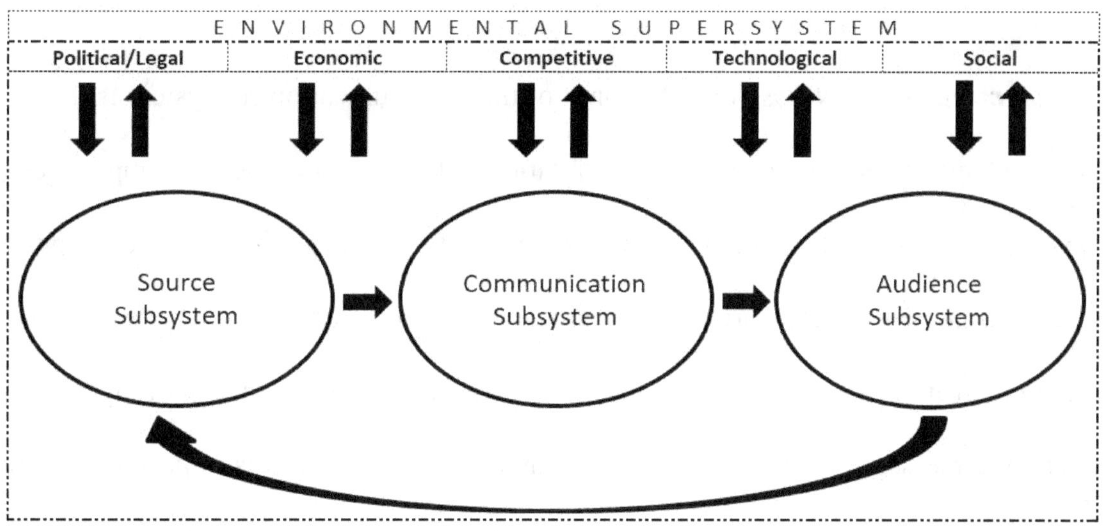


***Source subsystem.***  Models and process have to begin at some point in time.  For the APM, that 'starting point' is the input stage of the source subsystem.  It is here that the process begins.  The structure of the organization (or the advertising entity), along with its goals, management philosophy, and strategy determine to advertise based on various decision points such as a need to drive sales, desire to build a brand, and other rationale.  The organization's strategy is a key factor that influences how the process will progress.  These inputs then flow through to the 'campaign development' section of the source subsystem.  It is here that options are explored and assessed as to their relative benefits and alignment with organizational goals and priorities.  Research and analysis are (usually) conducted, and then, resources are evaluated and prepared to propose advertising campaign options.  The process then flows to the output section of the source subsystem which is known as the 'campaign recommendation.'  In this section, goals of the advertising are normally made explicit and expectations defined.  Further, specific audience analysis is conducted, and the tactical elements of the campaign are put into place as a part of the output of a campaign recommendation as well as final acceptance.  NOTE: In cases where an advertising agency is used, this would be the place where the client approves the campaign.

*Communication subsystem.*  The input of the communication subsystem is the output of the source subsystem or 'campaign recommendation.'  This flows to the throughput section of this subsystem, namely the 'communication process.'  It is here that the actual messages (advertising creative and copy) are developed, and appropriate media are selected for the advertising plan and, finally, where messages are encoded.  In the output ('messages') section, the advertising messages are transmitted to the intended audiences.  It is important to note that, unlike the PR process model, the APM separates the sending (transmission) of the message(s) into the communication subsystem while shifting the reception of the message(s) to the audience subsystem.

*Audience subsystem.*  The 'messages' (output of the communication subsystem) serve as the input for the audience subsystem.  The messages flow to the 'audience process' which is where target audience recipients (groups and/or individuals) are exposed to the advertising messages or appeals.  Message recipients either notice, pay attention to, or are / are not engaged

with the advertisements.  This is the point in the process where measures of delivery (e.g., AIM)

would be operationalized.  Finally, the output of the audience subsystem is the 'results' section.

It is here that the majority of metrics for advertising effectiveness are measured.  These

**Figure 4**

***Advertising Process Model with Subsystem Components***

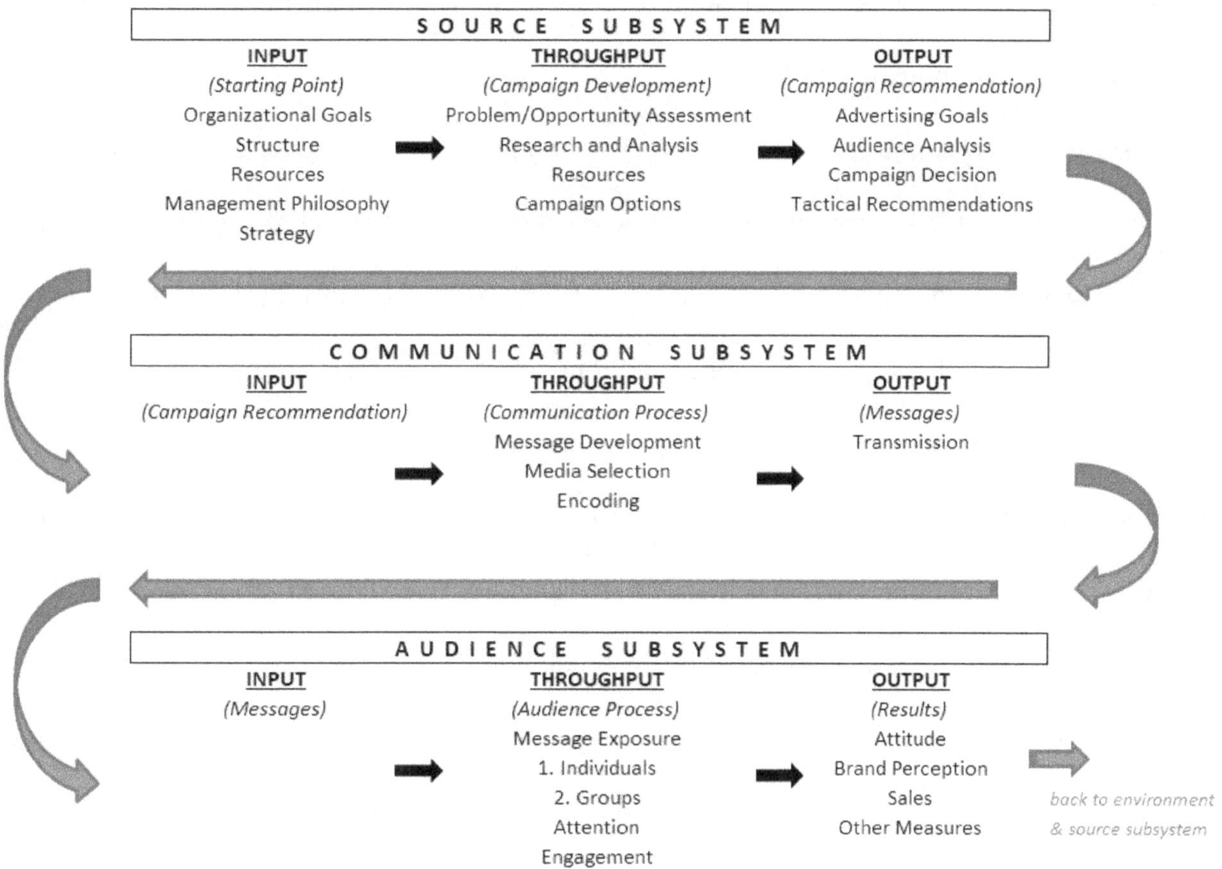


may include concepts such as maintenance or change in attitudes about the product or

brand, increase/decrease in sales, 'likes' – or other social media metrics.  Further, the audience subsystem in the APM is differentiated from the 'target audience' subsystem of the PR process model because it may not be appropriate to assume that messages will be delivered only to the target audience(s). Messages can be received by audiences that may or may not always correspond to the intended target audience. These additional exposures may have impacts that can be necessary for the advertiser to evaluate and understand.

But the flow never actually stops. This is a process. So, the advertising and downstream impacts from that messaging flow out to the audiences, as well as, the environment and back to the source subsystem. Further, it is important to note that all of the components and sub-processes interact with each other and can have effects on the environment just as they are affected by the environment.

***Initial model validation.*** An obvious first step for a model of advertising would be to check to confirm that it accommodates the basic elements of advertising. Several scholars have suggested important components that should be included as elements for building theory in advertising. Nan and Faber (2004) recommend four structural elements of communication that "are the unique elements that distinguish advertising from other forms of communication. Therefore, they should be considered in developing advertising theory and should be included in work that seeks to apply broader theories to advertising" (p. 16). These four elements are: skepticism, repetition, message coordination and a cluttered and competitive environment. Further, Thorson and Rodgers (2012) identified seven components that a message must include to be considered as advertising. They are: audiences, message sources, devices, media channels, advertising organizations, contexts, and messages (including both intended and unintended effects). Both the four elements and the seven components of are represented by the APM.

Nan and Rogers' four elements of advertising and Thorson and Rodgers' seven components of advertising are mapped to the advertising process model in Table 3.

By virtue of its design, the APM implies that there is a scope to advertising.  In other words, there are activities, concepts, etc. that are 'inside' the model and part of advertising.  However, there are also activities and concepts that are 'outside' the model – these elements are not advertising (although they may impact, or be impacted by, advertising through the environmental connects indicated by the model).  Although the systems approach acknowledges that boundaries are permeable, there are indeed boundaries.  These boundaries help define the scope of the topic at hand.

It is relevant to note that the APM does not attempt to understand the full and complete inner workings of the human brain.  The numerous psychologically-based attitude change and persuasion theories that have been applied to the study of advertising have attempted that effort for decades (and there are many who will likely continue in that vein).

**Table 3**

***Advertising Process Model / Scholar Concept Connections***

| **Advertising Concepts** | **Where the Concepts Fit Into the APM** |
|---|---|
| **Structural Elements of Advertising** | |
| Skepticism | Audience Subsystem |
| Repetition | Between the Communication Subsystem and the Audience Subsystem |
| Message coordination | Communication Subsystem |
| Cluttered and competitive environment | Competitive Dimension of the Environment and the Communication Subsystem |
| **Message Components of Advertising** | |
| Message sources | Source Subsystem |
| Audiences | Audience Subsystem |
| Devices | Communication Subsystem |
| Media channels | Communication Subsystem |
| Advertising organizations | Source Subsystem |
| Concepts | Source Subsystem |
| Messages (effects) | Communication Subsystem and Audience Subsystem |

Instead, the APM takes advice from Faber, Duff, and Nan (2012) and addresses other common and important aspects of advertising (while still accommodating psychological theories).

***Benefits of APM.*** An Advertising Process Model makes sense. There are numerous beneficial attributes to the APM. As discussed above, the model is appropriate for advertising because it utilizes systems theory as having a wide range of organizational communication studies and applications. APM is equally applicable in both academic and practitioner settings. Further, the model is parsimonious in that it represents a conceptually simple communication process (albeit customized for advertising). However, the APM is potentially incredibly heuristic in that it allows for virtually unlimited theory-building both up and out (to larger supersystems) as well as down and in (to contained subsystems) – as well as incorporating environmental dimensions. Despite the intentional non-focus on psychologically-based theories, the APM does incorporate those – in the audience subsystem. The audience subsystem allows for advertising research that focuses down to the minute level of the individual human brain (as well as collective or group processing/response). By the same token, the model allows for advertising research from broader approaches, including those at the larger group, multi-audience, and even the societal level. Moreover, APM is not media- or device-specific; instead, it can accommodate all manner of existing media and future media incarnations. In addition, the model is highly open to additional possibilities. Through its systems-based underpinnings, the APM is open to a host of influences from multiple aspects of the environment and variable inputs. The inter-relatedness of concepts in the model further allows for changes in model elements to affect the rest of the model and vice versa. This adaptability provides the capability for the model to evolve over time by incorporating changes (e.g., new media, additional devices, changes in the environment, etc.) into the approach.

**Limitations & Future Research**

This section discusses limitations of the study and suggests future research possibilities that might be pursued based on what was found in this study.

**Limitations.** This study incorporated a wide range of advertising practitioners and scholars to address the topic of cross-platform advertising delivery. It found that these advertising community representatives generally agreed with the use of impressions as a cross-platform advertising delivery metric. The study participants also expressed that there are significant challenges to putting impression-based measurement into practice. However, this advertising impression measurement (AIM) study has several limitations. First, a certain amount of bias is inescapable in qualitative research and this study may not have been immune to it. For example, one particular limitation might have been the author's high level of professional involvement and experience with the topic. However, this great familiarity with advertising and measures of advertising also provided credibility when gaining study participants and enabled more insightful and meaningful interactions with them in the interview process.

Second, the participant sample was achieved through non-random methods (author contacts plus subsequent snowball technique) which limit generalizability. However, qualitative research is primarily concerned with gaining in-depth insights and detail on the topic under investigation. Also, the interviews were conducted over a specific time period. In recent years, advertising and efforts to measure it have occurred in a highly dynamic and evolutionary/revolutionary media and cultural environment. Were the research to be conducted in either earlier or later years, the responses might have been different.

Third, qualitative research generally explores meaning and how people make sense of the world; as such, qualitative research is subjective. This makes it highly beneficial and, yet, the findings and interpretations are, in large measure, reliant upon the discretion of the author.

Fourth, this study used an incarnation of language (specifically, transcribed interviews) as the primary data source. According to Atieno (2009), inherent ambiguities in human language introduce the possibility of misinterpretation with qualitative research such as personal interviews. In addition, the topics discussed were relatively complex and did not contain well defined theoretic boundaries, further adding to potential misunderstanding.

Fifth, while the length of the interviews was substantial (averaging longer than one hour), more time to interact with the study participants might have yielded further insights, as might have follow-up individual or focus group interviews with the same or similar participants.

**Future directions for this line of research.** Several recommendations are offered for further research into this topic to expand and add to the understanding of advertising delivery.

The primary recommendation for future research is to build out and add to the advertising process model in order to fully reflect the needs of the broad advertising community. Efforts could identify additional variables and concerns and where they should fit in the advertising process model (APM). It should also be tested – including the opinions of both scholars and practitioners. As the model is systems based, it can respond to additional inputs and environmental impacts. This broader representation of the advertising process might offer a more holistic view of advertising to the advertising community.

As is often suggested, replication with more and different participants could help contribute to reliability and create a richer data set. For example, this study utilized mostly large advertisers; it might prove valuable to take a closer look at smaller advertisers. Expanding the sample might also enhance transferability.  Potential follow-ups might examine the questions and findings from this study using other methods of inquiry, such as focus group interviews.

Another idea for future examination would be to focus an entire study on the differences between practitioners and scholars with regard to some other aspect of advertising in order to explore the scholar-practitioner gap more deeply. The field must continue to do as Royne (2012) observed is the stated purpose of the *Journal of Advertising*: "to contribute to advertising theory and its relationship to practice" (p. 542).

In addition, the cross-platform nature of advertising and messaging must be recognized and embraced by scholars so that they can conduct theoretical research that includes appropriate levels of applied considerations.  For example, inclusion of multiple media where possible could enhance advertising research and potentially make it more applicable to practitioner community, among others.  Of course the author also highly recommends that future advertising research consider the impression, or delivery of impressions, especially across media forms, as topics of study.

Further, studies examining delivery measures (especially on a cross-platform basis) and those that consider message delivery – prior to 'effects' – are also strongly encouraged.  The scholarly community can ill afford to continue to limit its focus to psychological constructs and effects downstream from (largely assumed) exposure.  Understanding advertising as a process or a system could help direct research in this area.

Although not directly related to the focus of this specific study or the pursuit of particular, individual studies, yet another recommendation for future research would be to include panels of professional advertising practitioners as expert reviewers (above and beyond scholarly reviews).  While this could be considered somewhat heretical in academic circles, it might serve as one method to help bridge the scholar-practitioner divide.

**Summary**

In keeping with one of the themes of the study, conclusions are presented as key areas for the practitioner and scholarly communities to consider.

**Practical implications.**  The findings in this study seem to suggest two over-arching implications for the topic of advertising delivery: the need for cross-platform measurement and the obstacles to solving for that need.

First, the advertising industry – across all of its varied segments (including scholars) has expressed a clear and convincing need for cross-platform measurement.  The impression, as examined in this study, seems to offer a potential path forward toward addressing that need.  Therefore, it would be a worthy effort to explore studies to research, panels to debate, and committees to propose ways to implement and expand usage of advertising impression measurement.  For example, buyers and sellers might ask that their software developers and data providers incorporate impressions and impression-based buying into their platforms.  Further, agencies might present cross-platform delivery results to clients in the form of impressions across all media.

Second, the study uncovered considerable and significant challenges to implementing cross-platform measurement such as the impression.  Eight categories of challenges suggested by the participants of this study include vested interests, setting agreed-upon standards, comparison, data access, definitions, complexity of the media environment, relative valuations, and cost.  Seven additional obstacles proposed by the study participants should also be considered as challenges, including scale, data science vs. media & marketing, media evolution, walled gardens, creative content, fraud, and bright, shiny, new things. Collectively, these 15 challenge areas are formidable. But, the desire for efficiencies is also strong. Siloization takes many forms, but ultimately, it bogs down systems. Layers of vested interests serve to maintain existing monopolies, impacting revenue and restricting both data and innovation.

There are many potential steps that could be undertaken to address some of the challenges above. For example, standards bodies (such as the MRC) can continue to develop standards around impressions. Clients could push for open access to important delivery data. Entities of all flavors (including educational institutions) could invest in data science and media marketing efforts that work together. Further, investing in creative content that customers might really want to see (and possibly engage with) is a worthwhile endeavor to improve advertising.

Fundamentally, the advertising clients hold the golden keys; they can refuse to spend their advertising dollars with entities (media, agencies) that do not shift to holistic measures such as the impression – or provide reasonable access to data. If this begins to happen, then measurement providers would also be tasked by the media and agencies to provide cross-platform delivery in the form of impressions.

Thus, there is a communicated need – but also specific challenges that threaten to inhibit progress toward a solution. These are two important implications that this study has helped to delineate and categorize.

**Final remarks.** This study yielded several new practical and theoretical insights and conclusions regarding the challenges and opportunities to develop cross-platform impression measurements in the current and near-future media environment. Beyond these insights, three additional observations are worth noting. First, recruiting and categorizing the study participants into five groups did prove useful in several ways for this study.  Although considerable, the lack

of discreteness in the professional experiences (and responses to questioning) based on these

categories was somewhat surprising.  Both practitioners and, to some extent, scholars sometimes

migrated across group lines over time.  This exposure to multiple groups may have led to more

agreement in responses than might have otherwise been expected.  Still, participants from each

group offered many special or unique insights based on their experiences.  Second, 'siloization'

of media and measurement remains a serious and powerful impediment to change.  Fortunes

have been (and will likely continue to be) made in media – most often strongly fueled by

advertising.  Those who have current income streams are highly motivated to maintain their

positions and views of the best way to measure advertising delivery.  Third, discussions of value

(variable worth) in the world of advertising are still an important concern for practitioners

(although seemingly less so for scholars).  Concepts of value, including relative valuation of

media, are critical areas that are always considered in practice and should probably be considered

to a greater degree in scholarship.

Measurement of advertising using impressions (AIM) shows promise.  There is strong

support for this approach from participants across the advertising ecosystem.  In some ways, the

use of impressions as a cross-platform measure of delivery seems almost inevitable.  Meanwhile,

study participants agreed there will be significant challenges to overcome if that promise is to be

realized.  However, the impression may present an opportunity to overcome many of those

challenges.  For example, Wakshlag noted that advertising measurement needs to measure how

many, how long, and how often.  The impression, coupled with Ivie's potential de-duplication

solution would answer the questions of 'how many' and 'how often.'  If defined with a duration

component, the impression could begin to answer the question of 'how long' as well.

Advertising impression measurement seems to offer the simplest, most parsimonious, and most straightforward answer to the challenge of cross-platform advertising delivery measurement.  As Coutts (2014) observed, "the technology-driven age of big data is upon us, and the wise words of the 14th-century philosopher William of Ockham have never been so important.  His principle of logic was originally written in Latin as 'Entia non sunt multiplicanda praeter necessitate' and is translated in English to 'More things should not be used than are necessary'" (p. 741).  In other words, all things being equal, the simplest solution is often the best.  According to Kelly (2007), "Ockham's razor keeps you on the straightest possible path to the truth" (p. 20).  The impression, in all its elegant parsimony, may be that path for measuring advertising from a diverse, dynamic, and growing media ecosystem.

Finally, viewing advertising from a systems perspective presents a viable theory-building path to pursue – and the Advertising Process Model offers a first step down that path.  For the field of advertising to survive and thrive, scholars and practitioners must continue to explore cross-platform delivery in the dramatically changing advertising and media world.

**References**

Aaker, D. & Norris, D. (1982).  Characteristics of TV commercials perceived as informative. *Journal of Advertising Research, 22*(2), 61-70

Ad Age advertising century: Timeline: A 295-year synopsis of the most important events in American advertising, 1704 to 1999. (1999). *Advertising Age.* Retrieved from http://adage.com/article/special-report-the-advertising-century/ad-age-advertising-century-timeline/143661/

Assael, H. (2011). From silos to synergy. *Journal of Advertising Research, 51*(50th Anniversary Supplement), 42-58.

Atieno, O. P. (2009). An analysis of the strengths and limitation of qualitative and quantitative research. *Problems of Education in the 21$^{st}$, 13*, 13-18.

Babbie, E. (1986). *Observing ourselves: Essays in social research.* Belmont, CA: Wadsworth.

Baehr, K. J. (2005). Converged media ratings: Towards a new method of measuring media use (Doctoral dissertation).  Retrieved from ProQuest. (UMI Number: 3167382)

Baker, W. & Lutz, R. (2000). An empirical test of an updated relevance-accessibility model of advertising effectiveness. *The Journal of Advertising, 29*(1), 1-14.

Barnard, C. (1938). *The functions of the executive.* Cambride, MA: Harvard University Press.

Barnett, J.,Vasileiou, K., Thorpe, S. & Young, T. (2015). Justifying the adequacy of samples in qualitative interview-based studies: Differences between and within journals, Symposium: "Quality in qualitative research and enduring problematics" [Powerpoint slides]. Retrieved from http://www.bath.ac.uk/sps/events/Documents/27_jan_2015_slides/julie_barnett.pdf

Blythe, J. (2007). Advertising creatives and brand personality: A grounded theory perspective. *The Journal of Brand Management, 14*(4), 284-294.

Bogart L. (1986). Progress in advertising research? *Journal of Advertising Research, 3*(26), 11-15.

Buzzard, K. S. (2015). The rise of market information regimes and the historical development of audience ratings. *Historical Journal of Film, Radio & Television, 35*(3), 511-517. DOI:10.1080/01439685.2015.1052219

Caccioppo, J. T., & Petty, R. E. (1984). The elaboration likelihood model of persuasion. *Advances in consumer research, 11*(1), 673-675.

Campbell, R. H. (1965). A managerial approach to advertising measurement. *The Journal of Marketing*, 1-6.

Cannon, H. (2012). Media analysis and decision making. In S. Rodgers and E. Thorson (Eds.), *Advertising theory* (313-336). New York: Routledge.

Chang, Y. & Thorson, E. (2004). Television and web advertising synergies. *Journal of Advertising, 33*(2), 75-84.

Cheong, Y., Gregoria, F., &, Kim, K. (2010). The power of reach and frequency in the age of digital advertising: Offline and online media demand different metrics. *Journal of Advertising Research, 50*(4), 403-415. DOI: 10.2501/S0021849910091555.

Chmielewski, T. L. (2012). Applying the Elaboration Likelihood Model to Voting. *International Journal of Interdisciplinary Social Sciences, 6*(10), 33-47.

Christian, R. C., & Ochs, M. B. (1966). Audience measurement concepts for industrial publications. *Journal of Marketing, 30*(1), 59-61.

Coalition for Innovative Media Measurement. (n.d.). CIMM's eight criteria for solving cross-platform measurement of exposure to ads and content. New York, NY: CIMM. Retrieved from http://cimm-us.org/wp-content/uploads/2012/07/CIMM-Eight-Criteria-for-Cross-Platform-Measurement.pdf

Coutts, A. J. (2014). In the age of technology, Occam's razor still applies. *International Journal of Sports Physiology and Performance, 9*(5), 741.

Coyne, I. T. (1997). Sampling in qualitative research. Purposeful and theoretical sampling; merging or clear boundaries? *Journal of Advanced Nursing, 26*(3), 623-630.

Colapinto, C., & Porlezza, C. (2012). Innovation in creative industries: from the quadruple helix model to the systems theory. *Journal of the Knowledge Economy, 3*(4), 343-353.

Corbin, J. M., & Strauss, A. (1990). Grounded theory research: Procedures, canons, and evaluative criteria. *Qualitative Sociology, 13*(1), 3-21.

Corder, C. (1986). Adimpact-A multi-media advertising effectiveness-measurement method, *Managerial and Decision Economics, 7*(4), 243-247.

Cresswell, J. W. (2009). *Research design: Qualitative, quantitative, and mixed methods approaches* (3rd ed.). Thousand Oaks, CA: Sage Publications.

Creswell, J. W. (2012). *Qualitative inquiry and research design: Choosing among five approaches.* Thousand Oaks, CA: Sage Publications.

Cummings, H., Long, L. & Lewis, H. (1987). *Managing communication in organizations: An introduction* (2$^{nd}$ ed.). Scottsdale, AZ: Gorsuch-Scarisbrick, Publishers.

Danaher, P. J., Lee, J., & Kerbache, L. (2010). Optimal internet media selection. *Marketing Science, 29*(2), 336-347.

Danaher, P. J., & Dagger, T. S. (2013). Comparing the relative effectiveness of advertising channels: A case study of a multimedia blitz campaign. *Journal of Marketing Research*, *50*(4), 517-534.

Danaher, P. J. (2007). Modeling page views across multiple websites with an application to internet reach and frequency prediction. *Marketing Science, 26*(3), 422-437.

Dick, S. J., & Mcdowell, W. (2004). Estimating relative audience loyalty among radio stations using standard Arbitron ratings. *Journal of Radio Studies, 11*(1), 26-39

Duff, B. R. & Faber, R. J. (2011). Missing the mark: Advertising avoidance and distractor devaluation. *Journal of Advertising, 40*(2), 51-62.

EBSCOHost. (2016). Search for articles containing 'advertising.' Retrieved from http://0-eds.b.ebscohost.com.library.regent.edu/ehost/resultsadvanced?sid=f1571d9c-c913-4a7a-9670-05f79aef82f9%40sessionmgr101&vid=2&hid=111&bquery=advertising&bdata=JmRiPWE5aCZ0eXBlPTEmc2l0ZT1laG9zdC1saXZl

Elsen, M., Pieters, R., & Wedel, M. (2016). Thin slice impressions: How advertising evaluation depends on exposure duration. *Journal of Marketing Research*, *53*(4), 563-579. doi:10.1509/jmr.13.0398

Faber, R., Duff, B. & Nan, X. (2012). Coloring outside the lines: Suggestions for making advertising theory more meaningful. In S. Rodgers and E. Thorson (Eds.), *Advertising theory* (18-32). New York, NY: Routledge.

Farace, R., Monge, P. & Russell, H. (1977). *Communicating and organizing*. Reading, MA: Addison-Wesley.

Flosi, S., Fulgoni, G., & Vollman, A. (2013). If an advertisement runs online and no one sees it, is it still an ad?. *Journal of Advertising Research, 53*(2), 192-199.

Forrester Consulting. (2015). *Marketing relevance in an omnichannel world: How data and measurement are key to customer engagement. A Forrester Consulting Thought Leadership Paper Commissioned By Neustar*. Cambridge: MA. Retrieved from https://ns-cdn.neustar.biz/creative_services/biz/neustar/www/resources/whitepapers/marketing/marketing-relevance-in-an-omnichannel-world.pdf

Franz, G. (2000). The future of multimedia research. *International Journal of Market Research, 42*(4), 459-472. Retrieved from http://0-

search.proquest.com.library.regent.edu/docview/214809777?accountid=13479

Gambetti, R., & Graffigna, G. (2010). The concept of engagement. *International Journal of Market Research, 52*(6), 801-826.

Gangadharbatla, H. (2012). Social media and advertising theory. In S. Rodgers and E. Thorson (Eds.), *Advertising theory* (402-416). New York: Routledge.

Glaser, B. G., & Strauss, A. L. (1998). Grounded theory. *Strategien qualitativer Forschung. Bern*, 53-84.

Golin, E., & Lyerly, S. B. (1950). The galvanic skin response as a test of advertising impact. *Journal of Applied Psychology, 34*(6), 440.

Google Scholar. (2016). Search for articles and books containing 'advertising.' Retrieved from https://scholar.google.com/scholar?as_vis=1&q=advertising&hl=en&as_sdt=1,34&as_ylo=2010

Goulding, C. (2005). Grounded theory, ethnography and phenomenology: A comparative analysis of three qualitative strategies for marketing research, *European Journal of Marketing, 39* (3/4), 294 – 308.

Gruber, A. (1966). Position effects and Starch viewer impression studies. *Journal of Advertising Research*, 6(3), 14-17.

Guest, G., Bunce, A., & Johnson, L. (2006). How many interviews are enough? An experiment with data saturation and variability. *Field methods,18*(1), 59-82.

Ha, L., & McCann, K. (2008). An integrated model of advertising clutter in offline and online media. *International Journal of Advertising, 27*(4), 569-592.

Hazleton, V. (1992). Toward a systems theory of public relations. In *Ist Public Relations eine Wissenschaft?* (33-45). VS Verlag für Sozialwissenschaften.

Headen, R. S., Klompmaker, J. E. & Teel Jr., J. E. (1976). Increasing the informational content of reach and frequency estimates. *Journal of Advertising, 5*(1), 18-21.

Heath, R. (2009). Emotional engagement: How television builds big brands at low attention. *Journal of Advertising Research, 49*(1), 62-73.

Hirschman, E. C., & Thompson, C. J. (1997). Why media matter: Toward a richer understanding of consumers' relationships with advertising and mass media. *Journal of Advertising, 26*(1), 43-60.

Hise, R. T., & Strawser, R. H. (1976). Advertising decisions and the long run effects of advertising. *Journal of Advertising, 5*(4), 20-41.

Huang, C. and Lin, C. (2006). Modeling the audience's banner ad exposure for internet
advertising planning. *Journal of Advertising, 35*(2), 123-136.

Hunt, S. D. (2002). Marketing as a profession: On closing stakeholder gaps. *European Journal of
Marketing, 36*(3), 305-312.

Inside Radio. (2017). U.S. ad spend grows at fastest pace in 12 years. Retrieved from
http://www.insideradio.com/free/u-s-ad-spend-grows-at-fastest-pace-in-
years/article_735dbef2-0242-11e7-aa12-632d41a65863.html

J. Blackwell. (n.d.). 1935: The poll that took America's pulse. Retrieved from
http://www.capitalcentury.com/1935.html

Jenkins, J. L. (2013). A Qualitative analysis of the impact of convergence on advertising
(Doctoral dissertation). Retrieved from ProQuest. (UMI Number: 3592970)

Jessen, I. B., & Graakjaer, N. J. (2013). Cross-media communication in advertising: exploring
multimodal connections between television commercials and websites. *Visual
Communication, 12*(4), 437-458.

Johnson, B. T., & Eagly, A. H. (1990). Involvement and persuasion: Types, traditions, and the
evidence. *Psychological Bulletin, 107*(3), 375-384.

Jomini Stroud, N., Stephens, M., & Pye, D. (2011). The influence of debate viewing context on
political cynicism and strategic interpretations. *American Behavioral Scientist, 55*(3),
270-283. doi:10.1177/0002764210392163

Karlsson, L. (2007). Advertising theories and models: How well can these be transferred from
text into reality? (Doctoral dissertation).

Kast, F. E., & Rosenzweig, J. E. (1972). General systems theory: Applications for organization
and management. *Academy of Management Journal, 15*(4), 447-465.

Katz, D., & Kahn, R. L. (1978). *The social psychology of organizations*. New York, NY: John
Wiley & Sons.

Kelly, K. (2007). Ockham's razor, empirical complexity, and truth-finding efficiency.
*Theoretical Computer Science, 383*(2-3), 270-289. doi:
https://doi.org/10.1016/j.tcs.2007.04.009

Kernell, S., & Rice, L. L. (2011). Cable and the partisan polarization of the president's audience.
*Presidential Studies Quarterly, 41*(4), 693-711. doi:10.1111/j.1741-5705.2011.03910.x

Kerr, G. & Schultz, D. (2010). Maintenance person or architect?  The role of academic advertising research in building better understanding. *International Journal of Advertising, 29*(4), 547-568. DOI: l0.250l/S0265048710201348

Kim, K., Hayes, J. L., Avant, J. A. & Reid, L. N. (2014). Trends in advertising research: A longitudinal analysis of leading advertising, marketing, and communication journals, 1980 to 2010. *Journal of Advertising, 43*(3), 296-316.

Kim, J., Lee, J., Jo, S., Jung, J., & Kang, J. (2015). Magazine reading experience and advertising engagement: A uses and gratifications perspective. *Journalism & Mass Communication Quarterly, 92*(1), 179-198.

Kitchen, P. J., Kim, I., & Schultz, D. E. (2008). Integrated marketing communications: Practice leads theory. *Journal of Advertising Research, 48*(4), 531-546.

Koslow, S., Sasser, S., & Riordan E. (2003). What is creative to whom and why? Perceptions in advertising agencies. *Journal of Advertising Research, 43*(1), 96-110.

Kreshel, P. J., Lancaster, K. M., & Toomey, M. A. (1985). How leading advertising agencies perceive effective reach and frequency. *Journal of Advertising, 14*(3), 32-51.

Krugman, H. E. (1966). The measurement of advertising involvement. *Public Opinion Quarterly, 30*(4), 583-596.

Krugman, D. M., & Hayes, J. L. (2012). Brand concepts and advertising. In S. Rodgers & E. Thorson (Eds.), *Advertising Theory* (pp. 434-448). New York, New York: Routledge.

Laczniak, R. N. (2015). The Journal of advertising and the development of advertising theory: Reflections and directions for future research. *Journal of Advertising, 44*(4), 429-433.

Lafayette, J. (2015). Rentrak-Comscore Combo Turns Up Heat on Nielsen. *Broadcasting & Cable, 145*(34), 6-7.

Lafayette, J. (2015). Measuring TV Is Good Business. *Broadcasting & Cable. June 29, 2015.*

Lamoureux, D. (2016).  Advertising: How many marketing messages do we see in a day?. *Fluid Drive Media.*  Retrieved from http://www.fluiddrivemedia.com/advertising/marketing-messages/


Lancaster, K., Kreshel, P. & Harris, J. (1986). Estimating the impact of advertising media plans: Media executives describe weighting and timing tactors. *Journal of Advertising, 15*(3), 21-45. Retrieved from http://0-www.jstor.org.library.regent.edu/stable/4622106

Laroche, M., Kiani, I., Economakis, N., & Richard, M. O. (2013). Effects of Multi-Channel Marketing on Consumers' Online Search Behavior. *Journal of Advertising Research, 53*(4), 431-443.

Lavidge, R. J., & Steiner, G. A. (2000). A model for predictive measurements of advertising effectiveness. *Advertising & Society Review, 1*(1).

Learmonth, M. (2010). What Google Instant means for marketers: more ad impressions. *Advertising Age, 81*(32), 1-32

Leischow, S. J., & Milstein, B. (2006). Systems thinking and modeling for public health practice. *American journal of public health, 96*(3), 403-405.

Levinson, J. C. (1994). *Guerilla advertising: Cost-effective tactics for small-business success.* Boston, Massachusetts: Houghton-Mifflin.

Lewin, K. (1951). *Field theory in social science.* New York: New York: Harper & Row.

Li, H. (2012). Advancing advertising theories and scholarship. In S. Rodgers and E. Thorson (Eds.), *Advertising theory* (546-552). New York: Routledge.

Long, L. W., & Hazelton, V. (1987). Public relations: A theoretical and practical response. *Public Relations Review, 13*(2), 3-13.

Luo, X., & Donthu, N. (2001). Benchmarking advertising efficiency. *Journal of Advertising Research, 41*(6), 7-18.

Luxton, S., Reid, M., & Mavondo, F. (2015). Integrated marketing communication capability and brand performance. *Journal of Advertising,44*(1), 37-46.

Mandese, J. (2016). 'Digital" poised to overtake TV ad spending earlier than expected. *MediaPost: MediaDailyNews*. Retrieved from http://www.mediapost.com/publications/article/284577/digital-poised-to-overtake-tv-ad-spending-earlie.html?utm_source=newsletter&utm_medium=email&utm_content=readmore&utm_campaign=96327.

March, J. & Simon, H. (1958). *Organizations*. New York, NY: John Wiley.

Martin, L. & Medina, D. (2015). The economics of measurement. New York, NY: Needham and Company. Retrieved from http://www.capknowledge.com/research_reports/media_theme_research_reports/2015_06_08_Economics_%20of_Measurement.pdf

Marich, R. (2008). Measuring engagement: Audience metric exerts increasing influence on ad spending. *Broadcasting & Cable. April 26, 2008.*

Mason, M. (2010). Sample size and saturation in PhD studies using qualitative interviews. In
    *Forum Qualitative Sozialforschung/Forum: Qualitative Social Research, 11*(3).
    Retrieved from http://www.qualitative-research.net/index.php/fqs/article/view/1428/3027

Matricon, C. (1967).  A new index of advertising effectiveness. *Journal of Advertising
    Research, 7*(4), 33-39.

McDonald, S. (2008). The long tail and its implications for media audience measurement.
    *Journal of Advertising Research, 48*(3), 313-319. DOI: 10.2501/S0021849908080379.

McDowell, W. S. (2008). Why TV cume matters: An exploratory case study of four local TV
    news brands. *Journal of Media Business Studies, 5*(3), 1-15.

McGrath, J. M. (2005). A pilot study testing aspects of the integrated marketing communications
    concept. *Journal of Marketing Communications, 11*(3), 191-214.

McGuire, W. J. (1961). Resistance to persuasion conferred by active and passive prior refutation
    of the same and alternative counterarguments. *The Journal of Abnormal and Social
    Psychology, 63*(2), 326.

McGuire, W. J. (1984). Public communication as a strategy for inducing health-promoting
    behavioral change. *Preventive Medicine, 13*(3), 299-319.

Mersey, R. D., Malthouse, E. C., & Calder, B. J. (2010). Engagement with online media. *Journal
    of Media Business Studies, 7*(2), 39-56.

Naik, P. A., & Raman, K. (2003). Understanding the impact of synergy in multimedia
    communications. *Journal of Marketing Research, 40*(4), 375-388.

Nan, X. & Faber, R. (2004). Advertising theory: Reconceptualizing the building blocks.
    *Marketing Theory, 4*(1/2), 7-30. DOI: 10.1177/1470593104044085

Nowak, G. J., & Phelps, J. (1994). Conceptualizing the integrated marketing communications'
    phenomenon: An examination of its impact on advertising practices and its implications
    for advertising research. *Journal of Current Issues & Research in Advertising, 16*(1), 49-
    66.

Nyilasy, G., & Reid, L. N. (2007). The academician–practitioner gap in advertising.
    *International Journal of Advertising, 26*(4), 425-445.

Nyilasy, G., & Reid, L. N. (2009). Agency practitioner theories of how advertising works.
    *Journal of Advertising, 8*(3), 81-96.

Ohme, R., Reykowska, D., Wiener, D., & Choromanska, A. (2009). Analysis of neurophysiological reactions to advertising stimuli by means of EEG and galvanic skin response measures. *Journal of Neuroscience, Psychology, and Economics, 2*(1), 21.

Paine, K. D. (2009). Goodbye, eyeballs. Hello, engagement. *Communication World, 26*(3), 21-24.

Palda, K. S. (1966). The hypothesis of a hierarchy of effects: A partial evaluation. *Journal of Marketing Research*, 3, 13-24.

Patti, C. (1977). Evaluating the role of advertising, *Journal of Advertising, 6*(4), 30-35.

Patton, M. Q. (2002). *Qualitative research and evaluation methods* (3rd ed). Thousand Oaks, CA: Sage Publications.

Pearlstine, N. (2012). Brian Roberts on his vision for comcast. *Bloomberg Businessweek.* Retrieved from http://www.businessweek.com/articles/2012-08-09/brian-roberts-on-his-vision-for-comcast.

Pergelova, A., Prior, D. & Rialp, J. (2010). Assessing advertising efficiency: Does the Internet play a role? *Journal of Advertising*, 39(3), 39-54. DOI: 10.2753/JOA0091-3367390303

Performics. (2016). Executive summary: Advertising expenditure forecasts September 2016. Retrieved from https://www.performics.com/executive-summary-advertising-expenditure-forecasts-september-2016/

Petty, R. E., & Cacioppo, J. T. (1984). Source factors and the elaboration likelihood model of persuasion. *Advances in Consumer Research, 11*(1), 668-672.

Politz, A. (1975). The function of advertising and its measurements. *Journal of Advertising, 4*(2), 10-12.

Powers, J. O. (1903). Advertising. *The Annals of the American Academy of Political and Social Science, 22*, 58–62. Retrieved from http://www.jstor.org/stable/1009941

Preston, I. (2012). Human barriers to using theory and research on responses to advertising messages. In S. Rodgers and E. Thorson (Eds.), *Advertising theory* (529-540). New York: Routledge.

Reinold, T., & Tropp, J. (2012). Integrated marketing communications: How can we measure its effectiveness? *Journal of Marketing Communications, 18*(2), 113-132.

Richards, J. & Curran, C. (2002). Oracles on "advertising": Searching for a definition. *Journal of Advertising, 31*(2), 63-77.

Rodgers, S. & Thorson, E. (2012). *Advertising theory*. New York, New York: Routledge.

Romaniuk, J., Beal, V. & Uncles, M. (2013). Achieving reach in a multi-media environment: How a marketer's first step provides the direction for the second. *Journal of Advertising Research, 52*(2), 221-230.

Rose, P. B. (2012). IMC, advertising research, and the advertising discipline. In S. Rodgers & E. Thorson (Eds.), *Advertising Theory* (pp. 517-533). New York, New York: Routledge.

Rosen, D. (2013). YouTube's aggressive move into original content. *Filmmaker Magazine.* Retrieved from http://filmmakermagazine.com/68152-youtubes-agressive-move-into-original-content/#.V9n0W_krJUQ

Ross, C. S., Ostroff, J., & Jernigan, D. H. (2014). Evidence of underage targeting of alcohol advertising on television in the United States: Lessons from the Lockyer v. Reynolds decisions. *Journal of Public Health Policy, 35*(1), 105-118. doi:10.1057/jphp.2013.52

Rossiter, J. R. (2001). What is marketing knowledge? Stage I: forms of marketing knowledge. *Marketing Theory, 1*(1), 9-26.

Rotfeld, H. J. (2007). Is there a strategy behind buying advertising time and space?. *Journal of Consumer Marketing, 24*(3), 131-132.

Rotfeld, H. J. (2012). Adventures in misplaced theories. In S. Rodgers and E. Thorson (Eds.), *Advertising theory* (553-562). New York: Routledge.

Royne, M. (2012). Toward theories of advertising: Where do we go from here? In S. Rodgers and E. Thorson (Eds.), *Advertising theory* (402-416). New York: Routledge.

Rust, R., & Oliver, R. (1994). The death of advertising. *Journal of Advertising*, 23(4), 72-77.

SalesCast, SalesConnect [Video file]. Retrieved from http://www.twcsalesconnect.com/TWC/PB/SalesLanding.aspx?pageid=575

Schmidt, S., & Eisend, M. (2015). Advertising repetition: A meta-analysis on effective frequency in advertising. *Journal of Advertising, 44*(4), 415-428.

Schultz, D. E., Block, M., & Raman, K. (2009). Media synergy comes of age -- part I. *Journal of Direct, Data and Digital Marketing Practice, 11*(1), 3-19. doi:http://0-dx.doi.org.library.regent.edu/10.1057/dddmp.2009.13

Shachar, R., & Emerson, J. W. (2000). Cast demographics, unobserved segments, and heterogeneous switching costs in a television viewing choice model. *Journal of Marketing Research, 37*(2), 173-186.

Shen, F. (2002). Banner advertisement pricing, measurement, and pretesting practices: Perspectives from interactive agencies. *Journal of Advertising, 31*(3), 59-67.

Sheth, J. N. (1974). Measurement of advertising effectiveness: some theoretical considerations. *Journal of Advertising, 3*(1), 6-11.

Smallwood, E. E. (1992). Perceptions and resources: A test of the public relations process model (Unpublished master's thesis). Illinois State University, Normal, Illinois.

Soley, L. C. & Reid, L. N. (1983). Advertising article productivity of the U.S. academic community. *Journalism Quarterly, 60*(3), 464-542.

Smit, E. G. & Neijens, P. C. (2011). The march to reliable metrics: A Half-century of coming closer to the truth. *Journal of Advertising Research, 51*, 124-135.

Starch, D. (1928). Testing the effectiveness of advertisements. *Harvard Business Review, 1*(4), 464-474.

Stavitsky, A. G. (2000). By the numbers: The use of ratings data in academic research. *Journal of Broadcasting & Electronic Media, 44*(3), 535.

Steele, A., Jacobs, D., Siefert, C., Rule, R., Levine, B., & Marci, C. D. (2013). Leveraging synergy and emotion in a multi-platform world. *Journal of Advertising Research, 53*(4), 417-430.

Stern, B. B. (1994). A revised communication model for advertising: Multiple dimensions of the source, the message, and the recipient. *Journal of Advertising, 23*(2), 5-15.

Stone, R., & Duffy, M. (1993). Measuring the impact of advertising. *Journal of Advertising Research, 33*(6), RC-8.

Strong, E. K. (1925). Theories of Selling. *Journal of Applied Psychology*, 9, 75-86.

Taylor, T. (2009). Advertising & the conquest of culture. *Social Semiotics, 19*(4), 405-425.

Taylor, J., Kennedy, R., McDonald, C., Larguinat, L., El Ouarzazi, Y. & Haddad, N. (2013). Is the multi-platform whole more powerful than its separate parts? Measuring the sales effects of cross-media Advertising. *Journal of Advertising Research, 52*(2), 200-211.

Tsiotsou, R. H. (2013). Investigating the role of enduring and situational involvement with the program context on advertising effectiveness. *Journal of Marketing Communications, 19*(2), 114-135.

Tudor, D. (2009). Who counts? Who is being counted? How audience measurement embeds neoliberalism into urban space. *Media, Culture & Society, 31*(5), 833-840. doi:10.1177/0163443709339469

Tungate, M. (2007). *Adland: A global history of advertising*. London, UK: Kogan Page Limited.

Vakratsas, D., & Ambler, T. (1999). How advertising works: what do we really know? *The Journal of Marketing*, 26-43.

Varan, D., Murphy, J., Hofacker, C. F., Robinson, J. A., Potter, R. F., & Bellman, S. (2013). What Works Best When Combining Television Sets, PCs, Tablets, or Mobile Phones? *Journal of Advertising Research, 53*(2), 212-220.

Viljakainen, A. (2013). Show me the money! The quest for an intermedia currency in the Nordic countries. *Journal of Media Business Studies, 10*(3), 41-63.

Von Bertalanffy, L. (1972). The history and status of general systems theory. *Academy of Management Journal, 15*(4), 407-426.

Voorveld, H. A., Neijens, P. C., & Smit, E. G. (2011). Opening the black box: Understanding cross-media effects. *Journal of Marketing Communications, 17*(02), 69-85.

Wang, A. (2006). Advertising engagement: A driver of message involvement on message effects. *Journal of Advertising Research, 46*(4), 355-368.

Waller, D. (2005). A proposed response model for controversial advertising. *Journal of Promotion Management, 11*(2-3), 3-15.

Wang, Y., & Sun, S. (2010). An online advertising model: Comparing China and the U.S., *Journal of Current Issues & Research in Advertising, 32* (2), 101-115.

Webster, J. G., & Ksiazek, T. B. (2012). The dynamics of audience fragmentation: Public attention in an age of digital media. *Journal of Communication, 62*(1), 39-56. doi:10.1111/j.1460-2466.2011.01616.x

WFA (2008). *Blueprint for consumer-centric holistic measurement.* World Federation of Advertisers. Brussels, Belgium. Retrieved from http://www.wfanet.org/media/pdf/Blueprint_English_June_2008.pdf

Winslow, G. (2014). Efficiency now comes special delivery: Competition is heating up in the race to automate multiplatform ad distribution. *Broadcasting & Cable.* Retrieved from http://www.broadcastingcable.com/efficiency-now-comes-special-delivery/132727

Winslow, G. (2013). The measurement mess: New 'Frankenmetrics' leave monster of a task for Nielsen, TV networks and other stakeholders. *Broadcasting & Cable.* Retrieved from http://www.broadcastingcable.com/news/news-articles/measurement-mess/114643

Yunjae, C., Leckenby, J. D., & Eakin, T. (2011). Evaluating the multivariate beta binomial distribution for estimating magazine and internet exposure frequency distributions. *Journal of Advertising, 40*(1), 7-23.

**APPENDIX A: Interview Guide**

**Interviewer:** Ed Smallwood

**Participant:**

**Date:**

**Respondent Code:**


Thanks for your time today <INTERVIEWEE NAME>.  I'd like to get your opinions and insights on advertising measurement, specifically with regard to measuring cross-platform or multimedia advertising.


With your permission I would like to record this interview to ensure accuracy.  I'll also take notes to help me keep track of ideas or additional issues that may present themselves during the course of our discussion.


Your comments from our conversation today will only be used for this study.  With that in mind, I will be referencing and likely quoting specific comments in the final report.  Do you approve of these uses and agree to proceed with this interview?


<IF NEGATIVE RESPONSE, THANK THE PARTICIPANT FOR HIS/HER TIME AND END THE INTERVIEW.>


<IF POSITIVE RESPONSE, CONTINUE WITH QUESTIONS>

Thanks again for your willingness to be interviewed.

1.  Can you briefly describe your experience/background in advertising?

2.   How do you define advertising measurement; why do you think it is/is not important?

3.  What do you see as concerns with current advertising measurement?  <PROMPT FOR STRENGTHS AND/OR WEAKNESSES.  DO EXISTING METRICS BENEFIT OR DISADVANTAGE EITHER MEDIA, AGENCIES, ADVERTISERS, OR VENDORS?  HOW IS CROSS-MEDIA MEASURED?>

4.  What would be the benefits of a cross-platform message delivery metric that could be applied across multiple media?  <PROMPT FOR BENEFITS TO MEDIA, AGENCIES, ADVERTISERS, ACADEMICS, OR VENDORS.>

5.  How would you define "impression"?  Do you think reception must occur to qualify?  Can there be a "partial" impression?  <PROMPT FOR COMPARABLE VALUE OF IMPRESSIONS FROM DIFFERENT MEDIA.>

6.   How would you respond to the impression (or exposure) as a single, comparative measure of delivery across multiple advertising media?  <PROMPT FOR ADVANTAGES AND/OR DISADVANTAGES.>

7. What would be the challenges in creating, implementing, and adopting an impression-based measurement approach for multiple advertising media?  <PROMPT FOR CREATING/IMPLEMENTING/ADOPTING. ARE THERE CONFLICTS AMONG THE STRATA?>

8. What other considerations might be important for a cross-platform ad delivery metric?  <PROMPT FOR CONSIDERATIONS SPECIFIC TO THE STRATA REPRESENTED.>

9. In light of the dynamic state of media, how might advertising and associated message measurement need to evolve?  <PROMPT REGARDING INTERNET, SOCIAL MEDIA, USER-CREATED VIDEO, ALTERNATIVE DELIVERY MECHANISMS, AS WELL AS TRADITIONAL MEDIA.   WHAT ABOUT FUTURE-ORIENTED CONCERNS?>

10. How do you think your opinions might align with or conflict with those in different parts of the advertising industry?  <PROMPT FOR OPINIONS REGARDING HOW MEDIA, AGENCIES, ADVERTISERS, ACADEMICS, VENDORS MIGHT VIEW THE TOPICS DIFFERENTLY.>

11. Are there other issues or questions related to this topic that you think that I should have asked about?  <PROMPT FOR ANYTHING ELSE PARTICIPANTS MIGHT LIKE TO ADD TO THE TOPIC.>

12. Can you recommend 1 or 2 other people in the industry that I should talk to?  <PROMPT FOR THE 5 SUB-GROUPS: AGENCY/MEDIA/CLIENT/RESEARCH/ACADEMIC.>

Name: _______________________________________

Title: _______________________________________

Organization: _______________________________________

Associated Annual Billings: _______________________________________

Experience: _______________________________________

Media Specialties: _______________________________________

Industry Positions: _______________________________________

_______________________________________

Which area do you most closely identify with?  (Check one.) …and years' experience

☐    Buyer (Advertising Agency) _____

☐    Seller (Media and/or Representation Firm) _____

☐    Client (Advertiser) _____

☐    Measurement Community (3rd Party Arbiters/Advocates) _____

☐    Academic (Scholar) _____

Education: _______________________________________

Other: _______________________________________

_______________________________________

_______________________________________

# APPENDIX C: Participant List with Relevant Positions

**Buyer (Advertising Agency)**

| | | | |
|---|---|---|---|
| 1. | Debbie | Basham | SVP, Director of Audio and Video Investment |
| 2. | Richard | Fielding | VP, Director Global Research Group |
| 3. | George | Mafredas | Senior Partner, Director of Research |
| 4. | Robert | Winston | Agency Principal |
| 5. | Linda | Kahn | CEO/Director, Media Services |
| 6. | Kat | Pearson | Integrated Media Manager |
| 7. | Tom | Meyer | Media Research Director, Consumer Insights |

**Seller (Media and/or Representation Firm)**

| | | | |
|---|---|---|---|
| 1. | Jack | Wakshlag | Chief Research Officer |
| 2. | Trey | Harb | Director, National Sales |
| 3. | Susan | Brami | Regional Vice President, Advertising Sales |
| 4. | Marshall | Jacobowitz | Vice President, Audience & Product Insights |
| 5. | Gwen | Throckmorton | Head of Industry, Global Marketing Solutions |
| 6. | Nick | Garramone | SVP, eBusiness Operations and Research |
| 7. | Serena | Lal | Director of Demand Strategy |
| 8. | Art | Salisch | Research Director, Multi-Market |

**Client (Advertiser)**

| | | | |
|---|---|---|---|
| 1. | Blaise | D'Sylva | Vice President, Media |
| 2. | Andrew | Deming | Senior Communications Strategy and Brand Manager |
| 3. | Scott | Hawkins | Executive Director of Marketing |
| 4. | Denise | Dobyns | Senior Manager, Customer Relationship Management |
| 5. | Mary Anne | Moldenhauer | Senior Director of Media Services |
| 6. | Barry | Schrag | Director of Advertising |
| 7. | Brian | Johnson | Director, Advertising |

**Research Vendors (Data/Measurement firm or Advocacy group)**

| | | | |
|---|---|---|---|
| 1. | Sara | Erichson | Executive Vice President, U.S. Media |
| 2. | Jeff | Boehme | Senior Vice President of Television Research |
| 3. | George | Ivie | CEO and Executive Director |
| 4. | Joe | Matarese | Chief Technologist |
| 5. | Tom | Gombas | Vice President, Cable Division |
| 6. | Danielle | Zazula | Vice President, Business Development |
| 7. | Dennis | Buchheim | Senior Vice President, Data & Ad Effectiveness |

**Academic (Scholar)**

| | | | |
|---|---|---|---|
| 1. | Esther | Thorson | Professor of Journalism |
| 2. | Jameson | Hayes | Assistant Professor, Advertising & Public Relations |
| 3. | Harsh | Taneja | Assistant Professor of Advertising |
| 4. | Jennifer | Romaniuk | Research Professor, Marketing |
| 5. | B.R. | Duff | Associate Professor of Advertising |
| 6. | Sela | Sar | Associate Professor of Advertising |
| 7. | Peter | Danaher | Professor, Department of Marketing |
| 8. | Don | Schultz | Professor Emeritus In Service |